"Dr Davis demonstrates how a r combined with mindfulness exe making can be adapted to the int order to develop a beneficial appro practical importance for students a

—*Mary L. ...., ..., Licensed Creative Arts Therapist, Reiki Practitioner*

"As a practicing therapist this book is of great interest to me. Barbara takes me through each chapter, giving me the confidence to practice mindful art therapy and offer this mode to the appropriate clients. This is an exciting possibility for a therapist who has been working in the field for 25 years and I want to thank her for it!"

—*Marilyn Cobain, Private Practitioner Fellow of the Australian Psychological Society*

"I congratulate Barbara Jean Davis on her excellent book, which makes suitable reading for all health professionals and the public. It provides health professionals who work closely with patients suffering mental illness with a safe therapeutic tool for healing as part of their overall management plan. Barbara takes art therapy to a new level, by empowering patients to create art from a state of mindfulness and to tap deeply into their deep felt emotions that may be difficult to express, their own inner wisdom and cultivate creativity! This book inspires me to refer more patients for art therapy and to take it on for myself as a means of tapping into my own creativity through mindfulness!"

—*Associate Professor Dr Vicki Kotsirilos, Medical Practitioner, Department of Rehabilitation, Nutrition and Sport, La Trobe University and General Practitioner*

"Barbara Jean Davis is a master quilter of intentional mindfulness, art therapy and collaborative partnerships. In the book she creates her 'masterpiece quilt'—a unique 'nine-block' design for facilitating openness and engaging clients in processing experiences and developing insights. It is an inspiring resource destined to become a gold standard for practice."

—*Linda Thiessen, Founding President, British Columbia Artists in Healthcare Society*

Mindful Art Therapy

of related interest

Mindfulness and the Arts Therapies
Theory and Practice
Edited by Laury Rappaport, Ph.D.
ISBN 978 1 84905 909 1
eISBN 978 0 85700 688 2

The Ethical Space of Mindfulness in Clinical Practice
An Explanatory Essay
Donald McCown
ISBN 978 1 84905 850 6
eISBN 978 0 85700 510 6

The Compassionate Practitioner
How to create a successful and rewarding practice
Jane Wood
ISBN 978 1 84819 222 5
eISBN 978 0 85701 170 1

Shamanism and Spirituality in Therapeutic Practice
An Introduction
Christa Mackinnon
ISBN 978 1 84819 081 8
eISBN 978 0 85701 068 1

Focusing-Oriented Art Therapy
Accessing the Body's Wisdom and Creative Intelligence
Laury Rappaport
ISBN 978 1 84310 760 6
eISBN 978 1 84642 852 4

Mindful Art Therapy

A Foundation for Practice

Barbara Jean Davis

Jessica Kingsley *Publishers*
London and Philadelphia

First published in 2015
by Jessica Kingsley Publishers
73 Collier Street
London N1 9BE, UK
and
400 Market Street, Suite 400
Philadelphia, PA 19106, USA

www.jkp.com

There is an MP3 file of a guided meditation available with this book which
can be found at the following link: www.jkp.com/mindful-art-therapy.html

Library of Congress Cataloging in Publication Data
A CIP catalog record for this book is available from the Library of Congress

British Library Cataloguing in Publication Data
A CIP catalogue record for this book is available from the British Library

ISBN 978 1 84905 426 3
eISBN 978 0 85700 791 9

Printed and bound in Great Britain

Dedication

This book is dedicated to my late parents whose legacy to "see goodness in people and life around you" has led me to marvel continually at the first flower of spring.

Contents

PART THREE: Metaphorically Speaking

PART FOUR: Clinical Applications in Mindful Art Therapy

PART FIVE: Developing a Mindful Art-Therapy Practice

List of Figures

Acknowledgements

Figure I.1 Photograph of the sun

In 2011, we were visiting a beachside town on the South shore of Melbourne, Australia. As we came upon the ocean, we noticed a huge and intriguing cloud, the likes of which we had never seen. It was dark and menacing but even more compelling was the one next to it, which in sharp contrast was poised against the sun, luminescing. I quickly reached for my phone to take a picture. Simultaneously, the person next to me said: "you can't take a photo toward the sun; it won't come out." But had I not broken with conventional wisdom, I would have missed the opportunity to capture the image shown here, that may or may not have been part of the volcanic ash cloud that traveled all the way from Argentina to Australia. Committing to taking the photo was less about being right, and more about being open to possibilities. It's a matter of focus. And my intention was to capture the essence of this spectacular cloud for future reflection. That's just what art and mindfulness do when combined; they break off a bit from conventional psychology and open you to other possibilities for health and well-being.

There are many people who have lent their support in the undertaking of this book. First and foremost, I would like to thank my clients, not only those who are (anonymously) featured in this book, but all of my clients who have helped to illuminate my understanding of how to shape mindful art therapy. I have no doubt learned as much from any of you as you have learned from me in this undertaking. In seeing our work as collaborative, my sense is restored that the same energy that contributes to "dis-ease" can be transformed into resilience if there is the right opportunity.

In the task of conceptualizing mindful art therapy as a foundation for practice, there have been many casual and formal conversations along the way that have contributed to my ideas. In particular, I would like to thank a number of colleagues who have lent their support and constructive criticism. My sincere thanks go out (in alphabetical order) to Cheryl Leber, Ilana Rydaiski, Liz Davidson, Marilyn Cobain, and Roberta Honigman. Your support, wisdom and insights are greatly appreciated and valued, in addition to your friendship.

As a first-time book author, the writing process has not been without its challenges. My thanks go out to Maia Danziger and the writing group. I've gained a great deal of insight listening to how others shape the "worded world" and Maia's feedback has been valuable in learning about the writing process and helping to keep me on track. My thanks also go out to Jane Ginberg, who has supported the editing of this book and other written works over the past several years. A mindful and creative approach to the process of editing is no doubt a little out of the box, and I appreciate her enthusiasm to walk the talk.

And last, but certainly not least my heartfelt thanks go out to my husband, daughter, and extended family and friends for their ongoing support and encouragement, even in light of having to endure my ever-present mantra: "I'm on the computer!"

Preface

The recent paradigm shift from illness to wellness has led many people to seek alternative ways to reduce stress and enhance well-being. Countless self-help methods are available through books, the internet, and a multitude of face-to-face programs. While not intended to replace conventional medical or psychological intervention, self-help strategies can empower people with the tools to become proactive in restoring their health and well-being. However, as much as we would like to think there are instant remedies and immediate solutions to ease emotional suffering, the process takes time, patience, and often a measure of support.

Working as a psychologist and art therapist over the past several decades, I've noticed how contemplative methods facilitate the inward turn and help clients gain deeper access to emotions that underlie their anxiety and depression. Regardless of the problem in question, it has always seemed to me that the energy underlying anxiety and depression characterizes a client's suffering and needs to be addressed. It is to this underlying energy that mindful art therapy can guide clients inward to explore and express deep-felt emotions that keep them stuck.

Over recent decades, both art and mindfulness have become accepted within complementary medicine as remedial methods for treating medical or mental-health conditions (NICAM, 2014). Both of these age-old traditions have been used for healing. Although modern conventions often lack traditional commentary, secular methods that value the power of inner consciousness have begun to permeate health, educational and organizational settings. Studies now show that connecting more deeply to inner mental life can enhance mind–body health, and help people to address the pathologies that interfere with daily functioning.

When art therapy and mindfulness are combined, the two methods complement each other. As clients turn inward through meditative mindfulness they become calm, present, and observing of whatever is happening in the now. The shift from ordinary consciousness and pragmatic, everyday concerns toward inner mental life anchors people to the underlying energy that drives suffering. When suffering is observed through inner consciousness, clients begin to notice what they are feeling rather than being stuck in a victim mentality. This mental shift helps people change their relationship to suffering, which can then be expressed metaphorically through art.

Translating subjective thoughts and feelings into a tangible art form is empowering for those who have difficulty communicating their emotions. Where mindfulness helps to calm a person, art provides the liberating effect of enabling people to communicate through it. As clients become increasingly sensitive to their problems, discovery and deeper insights help bridge the gap between inner and outer reality (i.e., I want to make friends; I can't or don't know how to make friends).

The other day, while making a cup of tea, I noticed that the side of the box read "ethical tea partnership." I immediately saw a metaphor in how mindful art therapy also entails an ethical partnership between client and therapist to shape therapy respectfully, empathically, and remedially. It is to such a notion that I offer this book in the hope that you will be inspired to grow personally and professionally in the journey.

This book highlights the method that I use and a collection of case studies from my private practice working with high-functioning clients who experience debilitating forms of anxiety or depression. This highly adaptable approach will perhaps lead you to ponder on the method and read further, guiding you to cultivate a practice and develop a toolbox of strategies that resonate personally. Not an ad hoc approach, but rather one that sparks your curiosity and leads you to "re-search" how best to incorporate mindful art therapy in your work.

Book sections

Part One of this book introduces the background and theoretical underpinnings of mindfulness. This is intended to inform about the various perspectives and practical applications of mindfulness. Chapter 1 includes an orientation to the key features of mindfulness and how age-old wisdom traditions translate into mindfulness in modern-day therapy. Located within the broader context of wisdom traditions, secular mindfulness is viewed as a foundation practice for ameliorating stress and learning to refocus attention on present-moment experience. Chapter 2 introduces the neurological correlates of mindfulness, including an evolutionary perspective of the brain, and the ways in which mindfulness can aid neural integration. An art and science perspective follows that illustrates the neurological links that contribute to the method. The chapter culminates in a description of introducing mindfulness in therapy, both with and without meditation. These two types of mindfulness, though overlapping and emanating from the same age-old wisdom, are discussed in terms of their broader application in informing the therapeutic approach.

Part Two introduces a way of thinking about how mindfulness and therapeutic art can be combined. Chapter 3 begins with the characteristics of mindfulness and sets the scene for understanding the nature of present-moment experience and the inward turn. Also included in this chapter are the psychological functions of mindfulness and their overlapping features with art engagement. Chapter 4 introduces historical perspectives and comparisons of the way art has been interpreted therapeutically in the past. This leads to a discussion of how therapeutic art is integrated in modern-day therapy and then moves toward highlighting the overlap between mindfulness and phenomenological art therapy. The latter provides a solid foundation for blending therapeutic art and mindfulness. This is also the theoretical underpinning for my work with clients and research participants. Chapter 5 introduces the reader to a mindful art-therapy session. This is followed by a case study and culminates with a summary of how all phases of the session work as an integrated whole.

Part Three illustrates the method through case studies from my private practice. These are presented in Chapters 6–10. Part Four illustrates the method in terms of clinical applications across a range of conceptual and theoretical perspectives. Case studies from research and private practice are presented in Chapters 11–16.

Part Five introduces some ideas about developing a mindful art-therapy practice. Chapter 17 begins with the core foundation of relational empathy, followed by practical considerations to engage and accommodate therapist and client sensibilities. Chapter 18 provides the script for the guided meditation and music track included with this book, available online at www.jkp.com/mindful-art-therapy.html.

PART ONE

What Is Mindfulness?

CHAPTER 1

Introduction

This book introduces a method of mindful art therapy for practitioners across the helping professions. When words fail clients or they find it difficult to grasp or harness what they want or need to say, therapeutic art can provide another source of awareness, communication, and self-insight to guide the path of restoration and healing. When art is paired with meditative mindfulness, it deepens the inward turn and helps clients get to the heart of the matter more quickly. By inward turn, I mean detaching from ordinary, everyday thinking and turning toward inner consciousness.

Mindfulness is the active component of the mind in meditation (Mikulas, 2011), but you don't necessarily need to meditate to be mindful. In fact, as humans we have a natural tendency to be mindful, it's just that sometimes we forget how. Most of the time we move mindlessly through the day, getting swept up in old stories or multitasking that keep the "mind full" rather than aware and present. For example, we may get caught up in regrets about the past (contributing to depression), or worries about the future (contributing to anxiety).

This begs the question: "Does everything we engage in become engaging?" Langer (2005) in *On Becoming an Artist* suggests it can if we refrain from judging and accept whatever comes up without fighting it. When we are governed by rules, or how we think things should be, we become mindless to the subtleties of life that may otherwise lead us to be more open to change. But when we are open to creativity, we become more sensitive to context and perspective (Langer, 2005). As a corrective to preventing and managing anxiety and depression, mindfulness can be used effectively to teach clients to turn gently toward physical or emotional pain, and reduce stress through it.

These two ways to incorporate mindfulness sit well with art therapy: first, by incorporating meditative or contemplative methods to facilitate relaxation and deepen the inward turn for connecting with deeper consciousness in all phases of the art task; second, by introducing cognitive skills to bring clients into the present moment with what they are feeling. Not *how* (guilt, anger, shame), but *what* (I feel helpless, unworthy, agitated). Cognitive mindfulness also provides a skillful means for dialoguing with art, where remaining open and image-centered may result in deeper insights.

What is mindfulness?

Mindfulness is about paying attention to how things are in the present moment. John Kabat-Zinn (1994) has characterized mindfulness as "paying attention in a particular way: on purpose, in the present moment, and non-judgmentally" (p.4). Despite a myriad of overlapping definitions, most agree that when a person is mindful they are open, receptive, and fully engaged with what is happening at the time (Brown and Ryan, 2003; Chatzisarantis and Hagger, 2007).

Mindfulness is derived largely from Eastern philosophies and contemplative traditions. Buddhist meditation practices encourage concentration, clarity, and the cultivation of calm and positive ways of being as a way of life. In accordance with Buddhist philosophy, taking responsibility for our state of mind is the most important thing we can do to free ourselves of human suffering. Through a series of techniques to enhance concentration, clarity, a positive mindset, and a naturally calm approach to life, Buddhist meditation practices can provide an antidote to things like fear, anxiety, and confusion.[1]

In Buddhist psychology, the silent mind helps us to address emotional tensions through our five senses (taste, touch, smell, sight, sound). When we turn inward through meditation, we begin to observe inner consciousness (mind, body, feelings, sensations) with

---

1 See http://thebuddhistcentre.com/text/what-meditation for more information.

detached awareness. Stilling the mind aids relaxation. The practice often begins by paying attention to the breath while mentally scanning the body or repeating a word or mantra. As we shift from the ordinary, everyday consciousness to inner stillness, we may begin to notice our thoughts and feelings, as well as the environment around us.

In distinguishing "the mind" from "thinking," Buddhist practitioner Bodhipaksa explains that the mind refers to several modes of consciousness (thinking, feeling, sensing, imagining, moving, etc.) that exist simultaneously, whereas thinking refers to verbal thinking or self-talk.[2] But the mind is not blank during meditation, nor does the "silent mind" mean that we are not thinking. As humans, we are constantly preoccupied with our thoughts to the extent that we seldom notice what's going on inside the mind and body. However, from a place of noticing, we can learn to turn away from anxiety or the drama of why we feel the way we do toward what we are feeling. And by acknowledging, accepting and allowing these feelings to be there, we can begin to change our relationship to stress. Changing our relationship to stress is less about how we react to the outer circumstances of what's happening in our lives, and more about the way we respond to it internally. Despite habitual tendencies to overreact through things like fear, anger, or guilt, we can learn to detach from identifying with it and shift our attention to what's going on at present in the mind and body.

Even in light of this, mindfulness is not intended to "fix" anything, nor does it mean that outer circumstances will necessarily change, or that we need be complacent in situations that require taking action. There may be something we can or need to do to address a situation (i.e., develop communication or assertiveness skills). Nor will we necessarily like or want to focus on thoughts that come up (Hayes and Wilson, 2003). Human suffering is—after all—part of being human, and emotional pain is inevitable. What mindfulness can do is help us mentally distance ourselves from negative ruminations and learn to relate differently to the way we see, perceive, and respond

---

2 See www.wildmind.org/background/making-the-mind-go-blank for more information.

to life. There is no need to defend experience in mindfulness—we simply stop, notice, accept, and allow.

Although mindfulness is at the heart of Buddhist teachings, it can be practiced by anyone regardless of background or religion, through a range of contemplative or cognitive attentional methods. For Westerners who are inclined toward contemplative practice, secular mindfulness meditation can be used to aid stress reduction, reduce pain symptoms, and enhance well-being and performance. Although these interventions often lack traditional commentary, the common thread is in providing people with the tools to calm the mind and body, and gain insights into thoughts and feelings that guide behavior (Brown, Ryan, and Cresswell, 2007).

For those less inclined toward meditation, cognitive attentional mindfulness skills (training the mind to be present and observing in the here and now) provide a new angle for dealing with stress that borrows from age-old wisdom traditions. In contrast to conventional cognitive methods where problems are rationalized or disputed, cognitive mindfulness skillfully turns people toward emotions in a detached way that allows emotions to be there, without struggling or denying them.

Allowing negative thoughts to be there is not about condoning injustices or resigning oneself helplessly to difficult circumstances; instead, when we mindfully notice and accept what's going on, we stop trying to resist what happened or what is still happening and we can then begin to put things in perspective (Harris, 2009). Taking notice of what or why we feel the way we do brings focus to our internal dialogue and helps to transform negative or judgmental stories that we run over and over in our minds.

For example, instead of jumping to conclusions about meeting someone you recently had an argument with (annoyed; talked *at* me; didn't ask what I thought), you can learn to focus the mind skillfully on being present, noticing what you feel (voice constricting; neck muscles tighten; can't remember what I want to say). Learning to be present with anger, rather than getting caught up in it, brings useful insights about what you feel in anxious moments. The focus is on the internal landscape rather than on external circumstances, where curiosity replaces the need to get caught up in defensive attitudes or relive the past.

CHAPTER 2

Mindfulness Theories and Approaches

In accordance with various Buddhist spiritual practices as a path to reduce suffering (Hanh, 1976), secular mindfulness has been adopted in contemporary psychology to increase awareness, enhance coping, and reduce stress and maladaptive behaviors. Recent approaches and innovative psychological treatments have seen an increase in the use of mindfulness approaches and strategies. In behavioral psychology, neuroscience (the study of the brain and functions) is now contributing to these efforts, guiding our understanding about the effects of physical or emotional stress, and how we can learn to regulate it through mindfulness.

Neurological correlates of mindfulness

The balance of survival

In the balance of survival, the human brain has evolved to accommodate three core needs of safety, satisfaction and connection. To accommodate these needs, modern humans have what is commonly referred to as an old brain and a new brain. The old brain, often referred to as "the emotional brain," is known as the limbic system. The amygdale is situated in the limbic system, and is responsible for our basic survival, as well as for our emotional memory and reactions to things like fear or anger when we feel threatened. Five functions of the amygdale include motivational drives (like thirst, hunger, reproduction), appraisal (whether something is meaningful or not), generating affect (emotions and emotional states), differentiating different kinds of memory, and attachment relationships (Siegel, 2007, 2009, 2012).

In earlier times, when real tigers threatened humans, it was a matter of "eat or be eaten." Neurochemical transmitters such as cortisol are released by the autonomic nervous system (ANS) and ensured survival by activating relevant body systems and shutting down others to conserve energy. This was known as the "fight or flight mechanism" set off by the amygdala that enabled humans to flee or freeze in the face of danger. In normal circumstances, once out of danger, the parasympathetic nervous system (PNS) reversed the process by releasing neurotransmitters such as dopamine to restore homeostatic calm so that people were once again able to regulate physiological and psychological processes adaptively (Hanson, 2013).

The newer brain has evolved to include the cortex region of the brain. The prefrontal cortex is divided into the left (logical) and right (intuitive) hemispheres and is responsible for higher level functioning. Although they overlap in some tasks, each holds a predominant role in functioning. For example, the left brain is responsible for executive functioning (logic, reasoning) and enables us to make sense of the environment. It is associated with things like visual recognition, the retrieval of facts, speech and language functions, mathematical calculations, and processing music.

The right brain is responsible for our intuition and spatial reasoning. It plays a role in visual and auditory processing, spatial skills, and artistic and creative ability (Lusebrink, 2004). These hemispheres are connected by the corpus callosum, which communicates neural messages between the two. Neural integration is required for things like bodily awareness, language function, the modulation of mood, and the regulation of emotions (Cozolino, 2010).

A further evolutionary part of the brain that helps regulate emotions is the medial prefrontal and anterior cingulate cortices (Etkin, Egner and Kalish, 2011). These structures are located in the midbrain between the limbic and cortical regions and are responsible for emotional processing and regulation. In the balance between our thoughts and emotions, they play a regulatory role in moderating things like fear, anxiety, withdrawal, or conflict through the mechanisms of appraisal, evaluation, and regulation (Etkin *et al.*, 2011).

The difference between now and then is that modern humans are able to coordinate their responses to stress and directly affect restoration and healing (Porges, 2011). How mindfulness interventions can contribute is by teaching people to develop a coordinated response to stress; breath is used to calm hyperarousal, and bring us into the present where thoughts can be skillfully reappraised by the prefrontal cortex through intuitive and logical problem-solving. As research now shows, mindfulness, even if only used briefly, can generate a sense of physiological and psychological safety in which the body can repair, restore, and recover, even if only momentarily (Porges, 2011).

Make up your mind

When we refocus our attention mindfully, we can harness the power of change in both brain structure and functioning. Current trends in psychology are showing that mindful practices help reduce physical and mental-health symptoms, and enhance mind–body health. Cahn and Polich (2006) explain how the neurophysiological effects of mindfulness can help us reduce stress. Kabat-Zinn (1990), Davidson (2003), and others have found that mindfulness meditation reduces pain symptoms, depression, and improves immunity. Hanson (2009, 2013), Siegel (2007, 2012), and others have added to this argument in highlighting how neurological integration enhances resilience and psychological functioning.

Unlike conventional wisdom that believed our brains were fixed in early childhood and deteriorated from that point onward, neuroscientists now know that we can reorganize and establish new neural pathways across the lifespan (Doidge, 2007). As neuroimaging studies are beginning to show, the brain is fluid and plastic and how people behave affects the brain and contributes to our understanding about connections between the mind, body, and behavior (Dorjee, 2010). Increasingly, studies now show that regular meditation results in changes in the brain structure and functioning.

The process of neurological change refers to neuroplasticity. Neuroplasticity is the "capacity for creating new neural connections and growing new neurons in response to experience" (Siegel, 2010, p.5). Based on the notion that "neurons that fire together, wire together," mindfulness interventions have been introduced into therapy to teach people how to come back to baseline from a reactive to non-reactive state when feeling stressed (Baer *et al.*, 2006).

Recovering from emotional challenges and developing a greater tolerance of negative affect contribute to mental health (Farb *et al.*, 2007). From a functional viewpoint, learning to "respond," rather than "react," to stress enhances our neural integration (Kabat-Zinn, 1990). Neural integration is important to our well-being. As Joan Borysenko has noted, we have two minds in our brains: one that is reflexive, instinctual, and linked to survival (housed in the limbic brain); the other that is reflexive and self-aware (housed in the prefrontal cortex).[1]

The "wise mind" helps us to negotiate competing realities (positive and negative experience) that exist simultaneously in everyday life. When we react reflexively to negative stress, we become clouded and respond habitually without giving it any notice. It's automatic. But when we consciously choose to operate from the wise mind (through breathing, sensing present-moment experience), we disengage an overactive amygdala and neurologically shift from a state of reactivity to centeredness. This takes our awareness to the prefrontal cortex where, in the absence of reactivity, logic and intuition contribute to creative problem-solving and a greater capacity for resilience and change.

From the positive psychology school, Hanson (2009, 2013) similarly espouses that neurological integration is fundamental to coping and psychological functioning. In keeping with the idea that "neurons that fire together, wire together," Hanson explains how increasing positive awareness in our minds contributes to the development of new neural synapses. The more positive experiences we activate (by noticing good things, imagining positive outcomes, reflecting on our strengths), the greater the likelihood of fusing positive and negative neural sequences together. As we continue to self-activate positive experiences, we develop a greater capacity to

---

1 See www.facebook.com/joanborysenkocommunity/posts/101514946009 82429.

hold negative stress and positive feelings simultaneously without overreacting. This is not to deny that negative feelings exist, but rather to recruit a stronger, more adaptive neural repertoire to anchor to in times of stress.

From a mind–body perspective, the phenomenon of "rewiring" our brains has arisen in part out of the neurological and physiological enquiry into how images affect the brain and body (Malchiodi, 2003). As Malchiodi explains, the relationship between human physiology, emotions, and early attachment has given rise to this enquiry in attempting to understand the impact on our neurological functions across the lifespan.

Siegel (2007, 2010), from an attachment point of view, describes how being able to sense or name the internal world through images (even in the absence of words) aids neural integration and positively affects social and emotional regulation. For example, in the way mirror neurons can either activate anxious or depressive feelings or behavior in relation to another person, or be calmed through mindful attunement.

Porges (2011), from an evolutionary perspective, espouses polyvagal theory (PVT), which explains how the development of a myelin sheath around nerve axons enables humans to coordinate adaptive responses to stress, rather than shutting down to it. As such, Porges suggests that mindfulness interventions can help people learn to mediate unconscious ANS hyperarousal with greater skill toward developing positive social engagement, trust and, empathy. From a Buddhist perspective, calming is a functional response that cultivates rather than separates a person from the problem, where the focus is on the emotion rather than on the trigger. From a calm perspective, a person can safely express, explore, and understand their stress (Bien, 2006).

Badenoch (2011), from a standpoint of interpersonal neurobiology (IPNB), similarly notes how empathy aids neural integration. Under the broader rubric of mental health and well-being, positive therapeutic relationships are said to help comfort a client's hypervigilant state and facilitate openness. Through relational empathy and shared understanding, clients feel heard and validated and this often improves their understanding of emotions they may have grappled with for years. Furthermore, when clients become more informed through embodied awareness, they tend to become more self-compassionate and receptive to the possibility of change.

What's art got to do with it?

It has long been held within the field of art therapy that engaging in art bolsters several mental processes simultaneously. From an art and science perspective, Kaplan and colleagues have contributed to important links between neurological processes and art-making, for example, in attempting to bring an aesthetic understanding to inner mental space (2000). Here, inner mental space might be equated with the psychological lining of experience in psychology, or the content of the mind in mindfulness. To this end, Ramachandran and Blakeslee (1998) examine a universal grammar of aesthetics that focuses on rule detection and the essential details of an image. From a mind-body approach, Garai (1987) explores a unity of consciousness (conscious and subconscious processes) whereby art-making is thought to help structure emotional understanding.

Ganim (1999) explains that left-brain functioning is analytical and limited to understanding and verbalizing "what we think we feel," whereas right-brain functioning is intuitive and more directly linked to felt experience. Therefore, if talking about emotions is often hindered by defenses, the symbolic expression of feelings through art is closer to how we actually feel (Ganim, 1999). Lusebrink (2004) highlights some of these basic brain structures and functions that are affected by therapeutic art experience and intervention. She explains how the process of neural sequencing, as a natural progression from tactile-sensory experience to conceptualizing through symbols, aids perceptual processing through art, for example in providing alternate structural pathways for accessing and processing memories and visual and motor information.

Symbolic imagery in art engages sensory experience and enables people to "listen with their eyes" beyond the worded world where defenses keep them stuck (Landgarten, 1975, p.65). As Ramachandran maintains (1998), several brain mechanisms responsible for visual acuity are linked to the limbic system, which enhances sensation and ultimately survival. From a functional viewpoint, art provides a holding space for emotions where clients can more closely experience, structure, and control emotions through things like the intentional use of art materials, or taking safe risks (Ganim, 1999). Focusing beyond the ego or defenses helps people move more quickly into the core issues that threaten to overwhelm them or keep them stuck (Levine, 2005).

Studies in perceptual aesthetics contribute further to ideas about the link between sensory systems, recognition, and adaptive behavior. Perceptual experience helps us put things together; for example, in knowing how to put words into sentences or colors into an artwork (Calvin, 1996). This is through the neurological mechanism known as "sequencing" which enables us to structure experience into a coherent whole (Kaplan, 2000). Therefore when clients shape emotional experience through an image, it may signal an attempt to bring order to chaos.

Consider also the intimate link between the symbolic tools of art and language (Kaplan, 2000). Talking about emotions can be hindered verbally for those who can't find the right words or who are blocked by ego defenses. However, the symbolic expression of feelings through art can bring us closer to how we actually feel through neurological processes that are activated in art-making. Because symbolic images both generate and contain multiple meanings, their metaphorical qualities often extend beyond the emotional vocabulary available to fully describe it (Franklin and Polistky, 1992; Maclagan, 2001). Therefore, when a client says their artwork makes them feel depressed, it may be difficult to describe the fuller mood of depression in words, even though it may have become accessible through art-making. This reflects the silent power of art, which, like mindfulness, engages inner mental life through a range of neurological processes that extend beyond ordinary reasoning.

While these processes describe some of the neurological mechanisms that are activated by art, anecdotal accounts of the art experience, like intuition and connecting with spirit, have only recently been explored. Siegel (2009) for example explains that intuition is now finding its way into science as "the non-verbal information processing of areas of our experience, including the body, that come into our awareness and we can have access to them" (p.138). Achterberg (1994, 2008), from a complementary medicine viewpoint, has similarly explored how contemplative and spiritual practices through mental imagery, prayer, and other forms of traditional healing positively affect immunity.

Summing up

The capacity to appraise and reappraise negative emotions is significant and impacts on how we respond and express ourselves in life. For example, when "fight or flight" is activated in the amygdala, we typically react in accordance with previous neural conditioning. As such, the contingencies of recalling or generating fear (past or future; learned or imagined) can result in hyperarousal or anticipatory anxiety (Etkin *et al.*, 2011). The discussions revolving around art and neurological mechanisms further illustrate a range of symbolic tools for holding and processing emotions through art.

A threat, whether real or imagined, is in the mind of the beholder, and prolonged states of things like fear or anger result in hyperarousal. However, learning to be present and aware can lessen arousal so that feeling afraid or angry has less power. Although this process sounds decidedly simple, habits are powerful. They guide our behavior mindlessly through the same old routines. Even when we try to change our habits, we may find ourselves gravitating back before long to old patterns we sought to change. The common features of art and mindfulness as therapeutic interventions are in providing a focused awareness of deep-felt emotions and strategies for calming hyperarousal.

Both meditative mindfulness and cognitive mindfulness strategies can aid in emotional regulation. When paired with art they work collaboratively. These two types of mindfulness are discussed in the next chapter.

Clinical approaches and theories:
Two ways of approaching mindfulness

Two types of mindfulness are used in therapy. One is meditative mindfulness, the other is cognitive attentional mindfulness (minus the meditation). Despite their differing approaches, both derive from Buddhist practices, although they seek to reduce suffering in the conventional sense, rather than through Buddhist ideals of enlightenment (Dorjee, 2010). While meditation involves contemplative practice through inner stillness, cognitive attentional methods borrow solely from the active component of the mind in meditation, which is mindfulness.

Much as we may not like to admit it, clients often have only a limited number of therapy sessions according to work or government mental health care schemes or their private insurance. That is not to say that clients don't come to therapy beyond that point, as many do, while others prefer just three or four sessions. Accordingly, I tend to structure therapy by introducing the main tools of mindfulness and art therapy in the first few sessions. These can then be reinforced along the way, and also outside of the sessions.

From the outset, I typically introduce breath work and guided meditation for relaxation and deepening the inward turn prior to the art task. This enhances the focus and facilitates mental distance for clients to be present with experience. While I encourage clients to practice these skills at home, I have found that some have neither the time nor the inclination for meditation, but do find the skills of breath work useful in calming anxiety or depression in real time.

Other psychological educational tools that I implement draw on a range of mindfulness skills to help clients reappraise their life experience in positive, life-affirming ways. For example, instead of working with goals, I find it useful to work with intentions. Intentions require less striving, and are more about choices for everyday living than about serving an endpoint. I also introduce a range of cognitive attentional tools, depending on the client, which may include an Acceptance and Commitment Therapy (ACT) hexaflex (Harris, 2009) or scripts from positive psychology. These not only work well for dialoguing in therapy, but also contextualize image-centered enquiry in the present moment.

Contemplative methods

In a critical analysis of meditation and mindfulness in contemporary psychology, Mikulas (2011) has explained that when a person sits quietly in meditation, the mind becomes calm and the body relaxed. While ruminating, the mind has a tendency to cling to thoughts, feelings, perceptions, attitudes, and so on, whether they are real or imagined (Mikulas, 2011). Furthermore, concentration through meditative mindfulness aids relaxation by cultivating awareness on the content of mind, in a detached, observing, and non-judgmental way (Andresen, 2000).

Secular mindful meditation practices have been popularized over recent years by Thich Nhât Hanh and John Kabat-Zinn. In promoting meditation as a tool for physical, emotional, mental, and spiritual wellness, contemplative practices have since been adopted in medical and mental-health settings and industries for their health-enhancing benefits and positive leadership.

Mindful-Based Cognitive Therapy (MBCT) has emerged out of this trend as a non-pharmacological clinical treatment for depression and anxiety. In extending conventional cognitive therapies, MBCT turns clients toward rather than away from their problems from a relaxed, open, and accepting standpoint. Kabat-Zinn and Davidson *et al.* (2003) have found that weekly mindfulness training for ten weeks can produce positive emotions and enhanced immune functioning. Williams and colleagues (2000, 2002, 2007) have similarly found that mindfulness interventions can reduce the burden of depression and anxiety, and provide life-enhancing skills for prevention and relapse. McKenzie and Hassed (2012) also provided a user-friendly approach to everyday mindfulness in part as an integrative approach to health, and in part as training for medical students and health professionals.

But while meditation is restorative, it's not always sufficient to initiate change, nor will clients necessarily find or invest the time. This is when cognitive attentional skills can be used effectively to map onto cognition for positive change.

Cognitive attentional methods

Cognitive attentional mindfulness strategies can help to get people back on track. Although they seldom engage with meditative practices, the methods draw largely on mindfulness strategies that foster awareness and the skills to notice and allow thoughts and feelings to be there without judging them or trying to change anything. This differs from conventional cognitive behavioral methods in turning clients toward emotional distress with openness and compassion. Doing so aids the self-regulation of attention and a change in orientation toward a shifting array of thoughts, feelings and attitudes as they arise (Bishop, Lau *et al.*, 2004). Moreover, these skills transfer easily from within the session to real life outside of therapy.

The idea of turning toward rather than away from emotional pain is novel for some, and particularly for those accustomed to cognitive behavioral methods (CBT) that dispute "faulty logic." Disputing faulty logic seems a natural response given that we are hard-wired for survival; hence, the mind needs to reason about things in case it needs to shift quickly into safety mode. However, we often get caught up in self-destructive or self-sabotaging thoughts that keep us imprisoned in expectations or judgments. If we deny the deeper sense of these distortions, we are likely to dismiss the underlying feelings that drive our thoughts, feelings, and behaviors in maladaptive ways. Cognitive mindfulness skills allow negative emotions to be there, but not to overwhelm us (Hayes and Wilson, 2003). On the whole, clients learn to identify less with the stories, or what they do or don't like about life, and learn instead to reappraise negative experience within a context of what it means (Kashdin and Ciarrochi, 2013).

Proponents of positive psychology and Acceptance and Commitment Therapy (ACT) use cognitive attentional strategies and meta-awareness (simultaneously reflecting and experiencing) to bring people in contact with present-moment experience. Over the years, while finding it difficult to discern the difference between the two, I have nonetheless incorporated a variety of these techniques into therapy as a novel approach to guiding cognitive and behavioral change to enhance well-being.

ACT and positive psychology share common features, while they differ fundamentally in their approach and skill sets. However, both ultimately seek "to promote human flourishing" by introducing cognitive attentional strategies to enhance wellness and adaptive functioning (Kashdin and Ciarrochi, 2013, p.5). Although both incorporate a sense of values, ACT uses values as a foundation for purposeful action, whereas in positive psychology values can be used to represent the real from the ideal and become a pivotal point for therapy. Similarly, experiential acceptance (of private experience) differs in that ACT allows for it, but in the service of valued action, whereas positive psychology focuses on private experience in relation to mindfulness or emotion regulation (Kashdin and Ciarrochi, 2013). In the main, ACT and positive psychology complement each other and their differences determine how a therapist might decide to incorporate them. Overall, the greatest service of both seems to be in cultivating psychological flexibility that enables clients to overcome resistance to the mental patterns that keep them stuck. This sits well with art therapy in helping to maintain openness, presence, and curiosity through image-based dialogue and enquiry.

PART TWO

Mindful Art Therapy—A Method for Practice

CHAPTER 3

Mindfulness Processes

Characteristics of mindfulness

States and traits

Mindfulness can be both a state and a trait. A state refers to a reaction to something, whereas a trait is a more enduring quality of mind. Mindfulness traits are thought to contribute to secure attachment in adults (Siegel, 2009). For some, mindfulness is a new practice that needs to be cultivated, whereas for others it signals a natural way of being (Baer, 2006; Siegel, 2009). In general, mindfulness enables us to adapt to the environment and recuperate more quickly from stress. With regular practice, mindfulness states can be cultivated through meditation (Siegel, 2009).

Our tendency to think our way cognitively through problems is a matter of survival. We scan the situation through preconceived judgments in case we may need to go into safety mode. But when this happens, we not only overlook other forms of knowing, like our intuition or a hunch, but we can also get caught up in destructive or unhelpful thoughts. As Thich Nhât Hanh has pointed out, we have choices: "The more mindful we are the more we can choose which mental formations appear on the screen of our mind" (2001, p.18).

Being mindfully engaged is characterized by an embodied sense of enquiry. In contrast to analyzing what we think or feel about a situation, we explore the nature of it through thoughts, feelings, sensations, and our five senses. As we learn to distance ourselves mentally from judgments or expectations, we begin to accept things as they are, without trying to change anything, anyone or the situation. Confronting challenging life experiences or things that are out of our control can teach us to respond with compassion, flexibility, and resilience (Siegel, 2010). This occurs when we become more conscious of present-moment experience.

Consciousness

Consciousness gives us access to the world (Van Manen, 1990). When we think of consciousness, we typically think in terms of conscious or subconscious thought processes. However, we experience other types of consciousness that we often take less notice of; for example, when we feel 'downhearted,' get 'butterflies in our stomach' or have 'a gut feeling' or 'feel hurt.' Becoming aware of internalized body states allows us to *know* from a deeper place how stress affects our outer world. These somatic markers are accessible through mindfulness and enable us to sense a connection between mind and body and the impact on our lives (Levine, 2010).

Negative emotions get stored in the mind and body. When faced with negative emotions, there is a tendency to suppress or avoid feeling them. This is a normal part of coping and survival, but eschewing emotional pain in this way doesn't resolve it and can result in harmful or self-destructive behavior, or perhaps a tendency to overthink or distort reality.

As a preventive and corrective response to self-harm, foundational Buddhist practices can help to ease the burden of suffering and restore mind–body balance. For example, through breathing practices accompanied by simple mantras, or by establishing mental attunement through surrendered yogic breathing or nidra yoga that moves conscious awareness progressively through the body. Similarly, mudras (hand postures) are thought to hold energetic and conceptual meanings that restore physiological balance.

These age-old contemplative practices were designed to connect people with sensory experience and restore mind–body health through subtle forms of allowing. In everyday practice, they bring inner harmony and equanimity; during periods of hyperarousal, these techniques can raise consciousness and help foster regulatory effects in the mind and body. In secular mindfulness, we learn to allow awareness to happen as we move beyond the story rather than getting caught up in states of fear, guilt or anger. The deeper consciousness that connects us to present-moment experience is often mirrored in sensory experience. To coin a phrase, "the gift is in the present."

Being present

Buddhist practitioner Bodhipaksa (2014) has explained that the kind of thinking that goes on in mindfulness meditation is about reflecting. Reflecting inward is more focused and powerful when not clouded by a barrage of repetitive thoughts we run over and over in our minds. Instead, we become present with our thoughts, feelings, emotions, perceptions, and internalized images as they arise, but are not caught up or defined by them. We just notice and allow them to be there as we get comfortable with the experience of being present.

Being present tells us how things are, whereas self-observation helps us better understand how our thoughts, feelings, sensations, and judgments affect each other. (Bishop *et al.*, 2004). When we slow down and become present with what's happening at the time, we can witness worry and put it to rest, despite anxious or depressive feelings still being there. Being present also means that we can let go of the need to control our thoughts or defend experience, and learn instead to just notice.

Being aware

Being present and being aware are distinct but overlapping states of awareness (Siegel, 2009). Being present is the experience in the fullness of the moment when one is fully engaged across a number of conscious levels (mind, emotion, bodily felt sense, and the five senses). We can name what's going on in the internal world (sensations like feeling hot or cold, hungry, and so on). Being aware, on the other hand, concerns the experience of reflecting on being present. This involves self-observation such as reflecting on the experience that is happening in the present moment (I am putting on a sweater because I feel cold). But the sensory stream is the starting point of present-moment experience (Siegel, 2009). And so, I can observe myself putting on a sweater, but also feel the warmth it generates, the softness of the fabric, notice the color, and so on. As humans, we have the capacity to be present in our experience and reflect on it simultaneously. This involves meta-awareness (the ability to reflect on our cognitions, emotions, perceptions, and sensations simultaneously) and insight in addition to other characteristics of mindfulness (Dorjee, 2010).

Our natural ability to be mindful can be reinforced with practice (Kashdin, 2013). Relearning to become aware and reflexive can help clients learn to detach from painful emotions and moderate their relationship to suffering. For example, by learning to stop and notice what depression feels like, being present with it and accepting of it without judgment or expectation, clients can gain new perspectives. The key is to learn to shift from the contents of the mind to the process of the mind through appraisal and reappraisal (Hayes and Wilson, 2003). Shifts in perspective can be liberating for clients when they detach from over-involvement in the mind and instead begin to notice and explore what's happening in the moment. Through this, clients can learn to regulate emotions, or identify less with the judgments or stories that keep them stuck.

Breath work

Taking the time to be conscious and intentional with our breathing enhances mind–body health. Breath work is an integral practice in meditation, yoga, and qigong practices. It involves conscious breathing designed to center the heart and mind, and foster equanimity. From a functional viewpoint, conscious breathing connects us with direct and vital bodily experience that opens us to the senses, and connects us with inner mental life (Siegel, 2012). Conscious breathing increases oxygen saturation in our brain and body cells. Slow breathing increases heart-rate variability and enhances alpha brainwaves for relaxation and mental clarity. As a strategy for calming, the breath helps us gain composure, interrupt mind chatter, and refocus our intentions. The more practiced we are in calming down through the breath, the more familiar and attuned the calming response will become to the nervous system (Hanson, 2013; Siegel, 2009).

Although maintaining present-moment awareness can be a lofty ideal when we are hijacked by the emotions, a single, conscious, intentional breath can be grounding. For example, in stopping to take notice of what stress feels like, and then pairing it with a simple calming breath. This profound but simple strategy is effective in helping clients who tend to get caught up in strong emotional reactions or are affected by the aftermath of trauma. It's also portable; conscious breathing can be done anytime, anywhere, in real time.

Somatic markers

Learning to notice body sensations related to stress can interrupt a tendency to overreact to such stress. For example, when feelings trigger anxious or depressive states, we can teach clients to notice and stay with bodily sensations and ultimately distinguish across unique streams of awareness in the mind and body (Farb et al., 2007). Being able to notice and be present with what a strong emotion feels like—fear, for example—can interrupt the cycle before it runs rampant. This entails the development of reflexive skills. For example, in stopping to breathe (calming hyperarousal) and becoming present with fear, we can turn toward it and name the sensation (heart is pounding, palms are sweating). By naming the sensation, we engage a more coherent response between various parts of the brain that are activated by fear (the amygdala), and those which help us to recover from it (the prefrontal cortex) and make sense of it. As we conceptualize, we streamline a coherent response to what is happening (sensation), whether fear is real or imagined (appraisal), and how best to be with it (intention).

Ogden, Minton and Pain (2006) have contributed a framework for therapy through "the five building blocks of mindful attention." This includes an awareness of body sensations (much like Gendlin's 'felt sense' (1981/2007)) that turns one's attention to both fine and gross movements in the body, such as our heart beating, or our posture. Next there is a shift in awareness toward internalized sensory perception (taste, touch, smell, sight, sound), then toward a shifting array of moods and emotions, and lastly toward our thoughts. Although these building blocks were developed for trauma sufferers, they are highly illustrative of what mindfulness is as a therapeutic method: a means of choosing to direct our attention in adaptive and life-giving ways.

Intentions

Mindful intentions are about becoming aware (Siegel, 2012). When we set mindful intentions in keeping with the changes we want to make, we can begin to pay attention on purpose. For example, by setting intentions to be safe, healthy, and well, we may choose to drink less alcohol, eat healthy food, and exercise several times a week.

Intentions have purpose but they differ from goals that seek an endpoint which we may or which we may not reach, or may or may not be satisfied with in the end. Intentions are choices we make about behaviors that we continue to do to stimulate ongoing change. In contrast to striving to achieve an outcome, intentions are more about directing consciousness toward the desired change. They come from a deeper place.

As Siegel (2012) has pointed out, when we *pay attention with intention*, we stabilize our awareness and strengthen the mind and neural circuits of the brain. From a structural viewpoint, we set down new neural pathways that guide us toward health and wholeness. From a functional viewpoint, we are better able to access the inner resources required to accomplish tasks, stabilize moods, or regulate emotions.

Psychological functions of art and mindfulness

The philosophies of art and wisdom traditions both support the view that there is greater hope for emotional recovery when people stop, turn inward, and access deeper parts of themselves. Although the philosophies differ, they share qualities of openness and how we come to notice, observe, and explore present-moment experience (Rappaport, 2009/2014). When people are guided by an inner focus, there is greater access to the energies that fuel anxiety and depression through awareness of emotional and sensory experience. As contemplative mindfulness deepens the inward turn, images act as an anchor and signpost for communicating deep-felt emotional experience. As these parallel processes are cumulatively woven, clients can become increasingly sensitive to the energy and life patterns that drive emotional pain.

Mindful-based practices serve three main functions: to relax the mind and body, raise awareness about present-moment experience, and regulate emotions (Bishop *et al.*, 2004). The calming function of meditation aids relaxation, where decentering provides a psychologically safe context for exploring emotional pain. From within this active behavior of mind, we can gain deeper insights and awareness of how things are.

Drawing on inner resources through art has similar benefits: first, in helping people to access deep-felt emotions that may be difficult to harness or verbalize; second, in providing a means for cathartically releasing pent-up feelings; third, in providing a visual language resource for communicating such feelings; and fourth, in the power of direct experiencing that often results in inner mental shifts. In a remedial sense, engaging sensory experience, whether silently through mindfulness or art, or verbally through dialogical reflection, enables clients to capture and acknowledge the deeper essence of emotional life beyond the reasoning mind. In other words, we get to the heart of the matter, and what ails us.

In psychology, mindfulness is an intervention to calm the mind and body, increase awareness, and teach people to respond more adaptively and skillfully to physical or emotional distress. In art therapy, mindfulness methods overlap with the lowering of defenses and mental distancing by cultivating an open stance that enables direct experiencing through creativity. Taken together, the methods serve the psychological function of bringing inner and outer realities together into a tangible form (Silverman, 2001), for example when an image carries an emotional tone that a client can relate to, or conveys a visible benchmark for comparing other life experiences.

Art + mindfulness

Art and mindfulness have been used throughout time to heal, restore, and teach people how to live. Traditional art forms have played a significant role in fostering cultural identity and a communal lifestyle. Australian Aborigines in the west Kimberley for example animate dreamtime myths at corroboree gatherings through art, story, dance, and cultural expression to enhance social-emotional and spiritual well-being. Contemplative practices similarly offer a recipe for living, for example Buddhist methods that attempt to bridge inner and outer realities and foster the potential for positive change. Over recent decades, contemplative methods and art-therapy practices have been introduced into medical, mental-health, educational and organizational settings to facilitate healing and enhance functioning.

Both art and mindfulness practices support the notion that there is greater hope for spiritual and emotional recovery if people stop, turn inward, and access deeper parts of themselves. As Solso (1994) has said:

> It is being "at one" with the art; it is commingling a painting with universal properties of the mind; it is seeing one's primal mind in a painting...It is a level of cognizance that arouses profound emotions and thoughts, and yet is itself inexplicable. It touches us. (pp. 256–257)

The overlap

Although mindfulness techniques have often been incorporated into art-therapy practice, Mindful Art Therapy (MAT) (sometimes referred to as Mindful-Based Art Therapy) has only recently emerged as a discipline. Growing interest through research, practice, and various websites, blogs and discussion groups are beginning to show its efficacy. In Western society where recent trends are shifting from a focus on illness to wellness, the transformative effect of art therapy has found its way into medical and mental health settings as a valid form of complementary intervention.

Translating inner mental life into a tangible form is a hallmark of art therapy. But when art is paired with meditative mindfulness practices, it assists clients to access emotional pain in a more detached, open, and curious way. When we still ourselves in meditation, we turn away from ordinary logic or defenses of the ego, and move toward inner mental life where we can harness our intuition and deeper intelligence. As the mind quietens, the body becomes calm and we begin to notice a shifting array of thoughts, feelings, perceptions, and sensations that present themselves. The mind often returns to whatever commands our attention at the time.

Direct experiencing occurs when we focus on something—a thought, feeling, idea, or sensation—and occurs throughout all phases of mindful art therapy, including when we contemplate, make art, or reflect on it. From a psychologically safe and deeper state, the combination of decentering (mental distancing) and tangibly expressing deep-felt emotions provides insights into emotional blocks that are often difficult to express in words alone. As one consistently learns to observe and express emotions in this way, direct experiencing functions as the starting point for understanding the deeper resonance that underlies emotional strife.

As we surrender to what's there with openness and without judgment, we can begin to see things more clearly, just as they are. Sometimes we only need to acknowledge something, and without denying our anguish or sorrow, we can meet it mindfully and give voice to it through art.

CHAPTER 4

Art Therapy Perspectives

A tree, or not a tree: that is the question

In the absence of one single art-therapy theory, art therapists tend to adopt a range of theoretical stances to guide the therapeutic tasks and interpretation of the art. Many of the early art therapists who were pioneers in the field aligned themselves with a psychoanalytic approach, and assessed psychological functioning or diagnosed pathology through the art. Among these early approaches, therapeutic art was prized as an outlet for subliminal material and associated anxiety (Ulman, 1975; Cane *et al.*, 1983), the free association of repressed memories (Cane *et al.*, 1983; Naumburg, 1953), and as a method of transference (Naumburg, 1998). Consequently, therapeutic artworks were interpreted according to the psychological approach of the therapist, rather than from the perspectives of the client (McNiff, 1998).

However, theoretical orientations are varied and images seldom account for the multiplicity of processes in a client's inner world (Wadeson, 1973), or for art as a therapeutic process (Kramer, 1987, 2000). Moreover, the tendency to diagnose through an image can overshadow the subjective meaning. If we return to the notion of "a tree, or not a tree," we can begin to see how theoretical interpretations can be worlds apart. Consider for example a psychoanalytic framework where symbols are interpreted as expressions of the ego. In Freudian terms, symbols in art are considered to be repressed or sublimated projections representing urges, drives, or impulses of the ego. In Kohut's terms, there is an emphasis on self-structure where projective symbols characterize significant traits and dynamics within the personality. In Jungian terms, symbols are viewed within an archetypal framework of opposites alerting the ego to seek wholeness and integration.

This means that while a Freudian analyst might diagnose the structure of a tree within object relations (Lichtenberg *et al.*, 1992), or a Kohutian as a projection of parallel states of anxiety or depression (Liebowitz, 1999), a Jungian might do so in relation to opposing intrapsychic forces that represent tensions within a person's soul, voice, or free will (Jung, 1964). Although many art therapists subscribe to some of these approaches, others favor a subjective understanding and tend to lean toward humanist, gestalt, client-centered, positive psychology, or phenomenological art therapy.

In response to a growing field, Judith Rubin's seminal works *The Art of Art Therapy* (1984) and *Approaches to Art Therapy* (1987/2001) introduced both the art process and psychotherapeutic methods of art therapy as we know and practice them today. Consistent with my desire to refrain from pathologizing through art works and draw more on humanism, creativity, self-awareness, and personal growth, I came to adopt a mindful art-therapy approach. This method brings together into a therapeutic whole the core components of humanism (emphasizing values and personal agency), mindfulness (openness, awareness, acceptance, non-judgment), phenomenology (subjective and objective experience), and therapeutic art (expressive elements).

Phenomenological art therapy

Phenomenology is the study of how things appear in consciousness. The field of phenomenological art therapy was pioneered by Mala Betensky (1910–1999) to help people find the deeper meaning of their emotions through expression and creativity. In her work *What Do You See* (1995), Betensky explains how the aesthetic dimensions of line, shape, and color and kinesthetic expression serve art and psychotherapy.

Phenomenology involves a different way of "seeing" an artwork, beyond the obvious content of an image. Seeing in this way may enhance one's understanding of how visual elements of therapeutic art extend beyond words, and may help one access the deeper structures (meanings) of emotional experience. This is particularly useful for those who find it difficult to access or talk about their emotions.

However, because consciousness or that state of awareness tends to accept whatever we impress upon it, if we perceive life as negative, we are likely to be drawn to negative experiences, whereas if we see life as positive, we are likely to be drawn to positive experiences. Consider how this can be reflected in art.

Some years ago while teaching my hobby of quilt-making, I began to notice the parallels between inner feelings and outer reality. For example, if quilters were satisfied with the technical aspects of their work, they would often share positive life events with the person next to them, whereas the opposite occurred if they were dissatisfied with their crafts. Although this encounter with quilters was not intended as group therapy, I couldn't help noticing how conscious embodiment through the art form of quilt-making seemed to highlight the parallels between inner and outer consciousness: what people felt and how they anchored to life as a result of those feelings. Mindful art therapy is much the same where noticing can lead to new discoveries about matters of the heart and head.

Within phenomenological art therapy, the task is to remain open, image-centered and empathic (Franklin and Buie, in Franklin and Politsky, 1992), and to collaborate with clients to help bring hidden meanings to light in their artwork (Betensky, in Rubin, 2001). This requires a therapist or researcher to remain unbiased, free of judgment, open, present, and accepting to whatever appears. On the one hand, this might be describing the phenomenological attitude; on the other, a mindful attitude.

Phenomenology as a foundation for mindful art therapy

Phenomenology provides a basic foundation for mindful art therapy. However, as theories are often dense, lengthy and fraught with philosophical jargon, I have provided a brief summary below to simplify some of the basic considerations that inform theory and therapy. This list is by no means exhaustive, but provides a basis for understanding how phenomenology informs therapeutic art intervention, and overlaps with some aspects of mindfulness.

Considerations in phenomenology and art

WHAT IS PHENOMENOLOGY?

- Phenomenology pertains to how we experience the world through various modes of consciousness, including thoughts, feelings, sensations, perceptions, and actions (Spinelli, 2005).

- A core feature of phenomenological enquiry is "lived experience." Lived experience means "to live…[in] the immediacy of life itself as we meet it" (Palmer, 1969, p.107).

- A core feature of lived experience is that it encompasses "knowing" within present-moment experience. Inner knowing brings personal meanings, memories, and feelings together into a composite whole.

PHENOMENOLOGICAL ATTITUDE

- Both phenomenological and mindful attitudes share a discovery approach involving being with experience and seeing thoughts, feelings, sensations, and perceptions with openness and curiosity. Beyond any preconceived notions, therapists and researchers suspend judgment and explore what is appearing to their clients or participants.

HUSSERL'S THEORY

- Postmodern philosopher Edmond Husserl (1859–1938) explored the field of phenomenology as a theory of consciousness. The main premise is to shed light on the connection and flow between inner and outer consciousness beyond the understanding or confines of positive science.

- Husserl is often cited for the phrase "back to the things themselves." This means that how things appear arises from the essential nature of a person's thoughts, feelings, values, will, and striving. This is not "striving" in the motivational sense, but rather as it is conceived in consciousness.

- Intentionality is an underlying concept of Husserl's phenomenology that brings awareness to the object of attention (Husserl, 1927; Palmer, 1971). Husserl posited that intentionality is directional, where inner mental life is directed outwardly and purposely toward something. Intentions are thus characterized as both an internal awareness and an external event (Palmer, 1971).

- Intentionality characterizes consciousness and provides a structure for phenomenological reflection to clarify deeper essential meanings of inner mental life.

- Intentionality in art can be seen in the way a client attends to the art task; leaning in, keen or reticent, through their use of line, shape, or colors.

HEIDEGGER'S THEORY

- Postmodern philosopher Martin Heidegger (1889–1976) in extending Husserl's theory was concerned with the nature and existence of "Being."

- Heidegger coined the term "Dasein" to describe the simultaneous nature of everyday existence as it appears (existence) and appears to itself (reflection). Closest to authentic Dasein is its "lived experience" of itself (van Manen, 1990). In suggesting that human consciousness is a human's struggle to comprehend truth, Dasein imbues experience with sense and purpose through simultaneous conscious and unconscious processes that attempt to bring lived experience to light (Richardson, 1967).

- Heideggerian phenomenology is closest to understanding therapeutic art (Betensky, 1995). Heidegger conceived of art as a site for the happening of truth, set forth by a world of possibilities. Dasein (being-in-the-world) in its deeper realm presents itself by asserting or striving toward understanding. For example, where the formation of thoughts or ideas in contemplation lend themselves to the creative impetus and crafting of an image.

HEIDEGGER AND ART

- Heidegger conceived that the making of art brought out hidden meanings, where reflection on the art brought truth to the artist (Duits, 2004). As "a site for the happening of truth," art can both hide truth, as well as instigate tension between inner and outer reality. Owing to the multimodal nature of art, Heidegger set the hermeneutic (*interpretive*) task of interpreting art through the content and characterization of an image in order to grasp a deeper understanding (Palmer, 1969).

DIRECT EXPERIENCE

- Direct experience is a threefold process that includes contemplating, making, and reflecting on an artwork.

- "Poïesis" is referred to as a creative impulse (Knill *et al.*, 2005). Poïesis is a transformational process of changing something into something new and finding meaning in it (Thomson, 2011). Thus we go beyond the crafting of an artwork to "seeing" and thinking about its meaning through deeper reflection. For example, by considering the intentional use of art materials or the material handling of the work (facture) that may signal an inner need to take action, or another way of looking at things.

- Postmodern philosopher Merleau-Ponty (1908–1961) rejected Husserl's notion of subjective–objective directional intentionality and instead described the process as intuitive where *a priori* knowledge (that which is known) enables a person to perceive the whole gestalt and grasp "the invisible of the visible" (Flynn, 2004).

- Concerning art, Merleau-Ponty alluded to the totality of perceptual experience via the interplay of mental processes (visual, cognitive, emotional) that enabled one to "grasp all things" in the image. Furthermore, he suggested that embodiment through art cultivates rather than separates mind–body awareness (Maclagan, 2001; Merleau-Ponty, 1964; Flynn, 2004).

- We give shape to lived experience through the work, which in a sense makes artworks "lived experiences transformed into transcended configurations" (van Manen, 1990, p.74).

PHENOMENOLOGICAL REDUCTION

- Husserl introduced the notion of "bracketing." Bracketing means suspending judgments. In this case it refers to the therapist or researcher who should avoid imposing a personal bias or preconceived theoretical interpretation on the artwork. In essence, phenomenological art therapists and researchers play the role of witness and mediator in guiding the symbolic understanding of visual elements.

WHAT IS HERMENEUTICS?

- Hermeneutics means "interpretation" (Allen, 1990, p.551). Hermeneutics in psychology seeks to understand the meaning of human experience within its context, rather than within the confines of empirical science (Terwee, 1990).

- Hermeneutics entails a circular or iterative approach through reflexive dialogue and shared understanding. This informs a "hermeneutic circle" process through which co-constructed meanings between therapist and client, or between researcher and participant, can be negotiated.

- The primary hermeneutic task of phenomenology is to interpret hidden patterns and "ways of being" through form and structure (Spinelli, 2005).

- The primary task of phenomenological art therapy is "ways of seeing" structures of experience through visual grammar (Betensky, 1995).

- Hermeneutic methods in art therapy seek to understand reflexive consciousness and intentions. For example, reflection might focus on how an image first appeared in the mind's eye, how it was developed or modified, or how it came to be expressed through the form, line, color, and so on while making art (Davis, 2010).

- Or through the reflexive dimensions of the therapeutic dialogue during reflection where new meanings are co-constructed (Linesch, 2004). For example, in how reflecting on a particular color can imbue it with a vast array of associations or meanings; and also where two meanings converge, and the result is greater understanding than the sum of the two perspectives (Merleau-Ponty, 1964; Maclagan, 2001).

- Because art, by virtue of its nature, is open to both objective and subjective interpretation (Palmer, 1969), the psychological resonance through aesthetic reflection can become evident when a client's "personal symbology" (Landgarten, 1975) or style conveys a visible benchmark to compare with other experiences (Maclagan, 2001).

- For interested readers who wish to further develop understanding, please refer to "Additional Reading" at the end of this chapter.

The points above illustrate some theoretical aspects of phenomenology which inform therapeutic art and mindfulness as a method. These brief explanations serve as the pragmatics of mindful art therapy and the evolutionary processes that comprise turning within, mental distancing, engaging in reverie and art, and reflecting on the experience.

At the junction between contemplative mindfulness and phenomenological art, there seems to be a greater capacity for clients to grasp the essence of deeply-felt emotions, and begin to free themselves up from them. From a mindfulness perspective, as clients turn inward, they can begin to witness the core self, beneath the narrative of emotional reactivity or habits (Siegel, 2010). From a phenomenological art perspective, there are opportunities to re-perceive and express inner emotional life with imagination and creativity. These are discussed in terms of three core phases of the mindful art therapy method: contemplation, art-making, and reflection.

Contemplation

The power of mindful art therapy takes place in the comfortable silence of a relaxed and safe psychological space where clients turn inward through meditation and begin to notice inner mental life. Something happens when people quieten the mind, detach emotionally from their problems, and consciously connect in this way. It is as though they slow down, dim the lights, and let the real show begin. After the truth of these moments, clients have later remarked that they seem to gain clarity and focus, and some gain soulful inner shifts that guide transformation and healing (McNiff, 2004).

As with art, contemplative mindfulness moves us beyond ordinary consciousness toward the "psychological lining of experience" where a shifting array of thoughts, feelings, perceptions, and fantasies can play out (Maclagan, 2001). Mindful art therapy offers opportunities for being with uncertainty in psychologically safe ways. While this does not make life challenges go away, it does provide a context for gaining enough emotional distance to step back and witness emotional pain with sensitivity and compassion. As underlying cycles of anxiety or depression begin to break down through mindful attunement, art provides an outlet for expression and exploration.

Art-making

Consciousness comes to light through intentionality; for example, in envisaging the formation of an idea that subsequently results in crafting an image and making it tangible for awareness and reflection (Davis, 2010). Intentions reflect the actualizing tendency of making art where the creative impulse combines with the psychological lining of experience. In this sense, intentions might be said to provide an anchor for inner conflict, as well as a signpost for guiding clients to explore their emotions purposefully and creatively.

Creativity is essential for adaptive human functioning and comprises a wide range of "behaving, experiencing, perceiving and communicating" (Maslow, 1971). Being creative means "being able to work with what exists in the moment...and to bring something new into being" (Oyan, 2003, p.66). Creativity, whether through imaginative play, art-based endeavors or ordinary tasks like cooking or washing the dishes, offers a holding environment for reverie where we can engage in our natural propensity for daydreaming and imagination. The parallel process of distancing oneself from ordinary logic (decentering), and cultivating openness through creativity, opens clients up to endless possibilities.

Working with symbolic images helps clients to structure their feelings through the neural substructures linking language and emotions (Kramer, 2000), and sensory experience (Lusebrink, 2004). The need to do so in the absence of dialogue may arise out of an inability to communicate, or because a problem is either too sensitive or painful to discuss. Nonetheless, the silent power of art through direct experiencing can contribute to positive mental shifts in the psyche and, in some instances, it replaces the need to talk (Betensky, 1995; Kramer, 2001; Rubin, 2005).

Expression brings form and content together and is therefore the most important element in phenomenological art therapy (Betensky, 1995). Expressive engagement can open clients to endless possibilities through art. Clients can use their favorite colors or styles in whatever ways make sense to them, or they can try something different. Furthermore, because therapeutic art does not entail the critical evaluation of fine art, clients can approach the work intentionally, sensibly, and imaginatively without fear of judgment.

Aesthetics in therapeutic art is not commensurable with the Kantian sense of fine art or beauty, although a client's artwork may indeed be beautiful. Here aesthetics refers to the structural features of line, shape, or color that comprise a visual account of what's going on in inner mental life (Betensky, 1995). These visual elements often signal rich sources of material that may not readily be put into words, but are communicated through symbols, gesture, or tone in an artwork (Lark, 2005).

Sigmund Koch (in Franklin, 2001) has investigated the creative impulse of artists across the professions (fine art, music, performers, choreographers). He has found that artists seek a "deeper human context" in which they explore human calamity. From a therapeutic viewpoint, aesthetics captures the form of the artwork as well as the therapeutic process and energy a client brings to the experience. For example, visual and neurological perception works collaboratively in memory through the familiarity of shapes (Arnheim, 1969).

Therefore, perceptual aesthetics contributes to the idea of how art may forge links between memory, recognition, sensory information, and adaptive behaviors.

Reflecting

The idea of phenomenological intuiting derives from expressionist art theory. Arnheim's (1969) approach to intuiting was to see the artwork beyond its face value or its arrangement of lines, shapes or colors to explore aesthetic perception in the tensions in the work. These tensions are thought to mirror other domains of experience (Arnheim, 1969; Betensky, 1995). Thus, perceiving might be equated with thinking, reasoning with intuition, and observation with invention. Furthermore, beyond the mechanics of visual processing is the deeper grasp of significant structural patterns (meanings) (Arnheim, 1969).

The interpretive method of phenomenological intuiting is image-centered where all modes of expression come together to highlight contrasts between inner and outer reality (Betensky, 1995; Linesch, 1994). With an emphasis on a non-judgmental approach, reflections are grounded in visual, verbal, and non-verbal expression. As expression is important to the phenomenological approach, images provide a springboard for understanding a client's world.

Guiding clients toward rather than away from their artwork is in some ways similar to cognitive mindful appraisal where clients approach emotional pain with presence, openness, and curiosity. Approaching images in this way enables both client and therapist to see the artwork afresh, and dialogue beyond its face value, in terms of the underlying meaning expressed in for example the liveliness or tensions of line, color, and shape or form, or through the deeper emotional tone of a work.

Aesthetic reflection therefore helps to construe meaning from the visual elements of a work (Arnheim, 1992). Furthermore, it is the basis for engaging image-based enquiry and interpretation for practice and research (McNiff, 2004). As such, we can begin to see contrasts between inner and outer reality in the aesthetic structures of an image, or perhaps inconsistencies. These are often revealed through the kinesthetic structure of an artwork. For example, a client may appear not to mind too much about a particular issue while talking about it, but may then put considerable energy and deliberation into the work (through form, color, or tensions), thereby showing the discrepancies between the real and ideal experience. In the following case study, the aesthetic dimensions of this client's artwork served as both an anchor and signpost for expressing her emotions and organizing her thinking.

Connecting the dots

Sally

Sally was a 20-year-old design student who would soon finish her course. Feeling at a loose end, she was also experiencing relationship issues which further contributed to her angst and confusion. Describing herself as self-sufficient, Sally had a need for structure and control over her life. Uncertainty made her feel anxious, and so she came to therapy to work things out.

Given her design background, Sally found it easy to explore her thoughts through lines, angles, and geometric shapes. In a task on alternate perspectives, she drew four stylized trees, identical in shape, which she said resembled a Pac-Man she'd seen in a movie earlier that week. This task was very much about using art as a creative solution to help Sally meet her feelings of uncertainty, and begin to move forward.

The first of these drawings was solid green representing a realistic tree, and the second was solid black, which was more in keeping with a trendy design aesthetic. She then experimented with a third that she said "looked terrible…and had an ugly blue" which she subsequently threw away. However, the fourth, which is pictured here on the right alongside her fifth, seemed to mark a shift in her emotional involvement with the exercise.

Sally mentioned that this tree stood out the most. She said that "it had red…like a stop sign…and I [realized I]…hadn't been in such a mess since when my business failed…this tree gave a view of everything…" (at the time, this seemed to mark her inner tensions and the essential nature of her quandary). Feeling satisfied with her work and as though she had gained some valuable insight, Sally lifted her drawing from the table to discover the paper underneath, which she found intriguing.

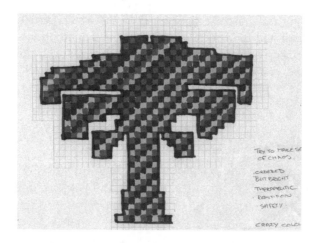

Figure 4.1 Sally 1: Trees (see color plate)

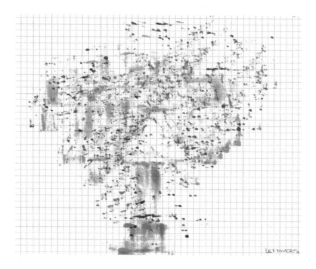

Figure 4.2 Sally 2: Trees (see color plate)

This second image, shown on the left, Sally described as "a maze of dots…representing the leftovers." This insight appealed to Sally as the "organic foundation" of the task, which led to self-discovery and the recognition that structure comes from chaos, and that there may be other possibilities she hadn't yet considered.

In terms of consciousness where the mind functions as a whole, Sally's response to this image seemed to bring perception together with intuition where she was able to metaphorically connect the dots in her mind and grasp the significance of the whole (Arnheim, 1969). This hidden and unexpected work became a method for releasing, acknowledging, and transforming negative feelings to a point where Sally could come closer to resolving her issues and felt ready to move on.

Summing up

This task on alternate perspectives was about using art as a creative solution to free Sally from feeling stuck and anxious. Interestingly, clients during these sorts of art tasks commonly express the organic nature of trees, combined with interpretive reflections associated with personal growth. Along these lines, Sally's trees progressively moved from realistic to being "crazy" with the colors of the third tree that she found challenging, and then to a more complete horizon of ideas where she gained valuable insights into both the presence and absence of experience through her images. Taking risks in art enabled Sally to see how far away from control she was ready to venture out. She destroyed the "crazy" tree in favor of redrawing it to maintain a balance between venturing outside of the norm, while maintaining boundaries that were acceptable.

Although the stylized form of the trees matched Sally's sensibilities as a design student, the unstructured maze of dots— the leftovers—spoke to her on a deeper level. Feeling initially challenged by her need for rules and boundaries, these "leftovers" were compelling, and marked a discovery phase which helped Sally begin to accept her feelings of ambiguity. Phenomenological intuiting through openness and discovery aided this task in guiding Sally to find the deeper resonance of those feelings and to consider other alternatives. In reminiscing about an earlier weaving phase, where Sally typically "wove ideas and relationships into scarves," she spontaneously produced a drawing of a weaving which helped her structure a more flexible plan around the choices she needed to make.

CHAPTER 5

Inside a Mindful Art Therapy Session

When we distance ourselves from ordinary thought, we can begin to transform feeling sad, worried, angry or afraid into wondering about it. Children tend to do this naturally without much concern. But as we get older, we often lose sight of our capacity for creativity and instead become fixed in limiting beliefs that often rob us of our vitality or thwart our capacity to thrive. As one client described:

> When we are born, we are the essence of who we are. Then life adds its expectations and burdens, and thus reshapes us. As we age into adulthood and search for meaning, we try to strip away these limitations and what's been added so that we can return to who we are: our authentic self. It's a visual thing; like a sculptor chipping away the outer surface.

From an observing rather than a striving stance, we can learn to acknowledge and accept things as they are, without trying to change anything. When we accept things as they are, we stop struggling. When we stop struggling, we are in a more powerful position to make wise and thoughtful choices. Sometimes it is a matter of choosing to let go of outdated emotional baggage and just let things be; at other times, the situation may require skilling up to enhance effective coping or resilience. We develop skills for coping with life as we go along, yet most of us are seldom taught to just let the mind settle and see what we can make of it. Mindfulness allows for this.

In working with high-functioning clients who experience debilitating forms of anxiety and depression, I have found that meditative mindfulness combined with therapeutic art tasks help clients to access and free up emotional blocks. Clients tend to focus more easily through the method, with less attachment and greater awareness than in talk therapy alone, or when engaging in art tasks without mindfulness.

As a quilter, it's hard to resist not laying out the pieces of a project to see how they go together. It's the same whether working with cloth or with the theoretical pieces that make up a lecture, workshop, or other academic project. The important thing is to be open enough to explore how these methods can, will, or might fit together. The process is essentially mindful in allowing various elements to flow across one another reflexively. Figure 5.1 shows how various elements of mindful art therapy (contemplating, making, reflecting) come together into a single mode of receptivity and engagement in a therapy session.

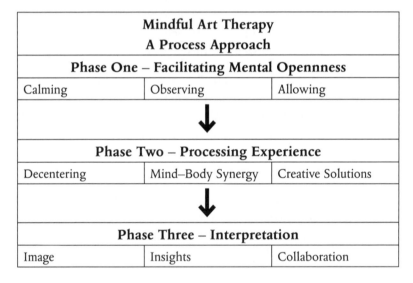

Mindful Art Therapy A Process Approach		
Phase One – Facilitating Mental Opennness		
Calming	Observing	Allowing
↓		
Phase Two – Processing Experience		
Decentering	Mind–Body Synergy	Creative Solutions
↓		
Phase Three – Interpretation		
Image	Insights	Collaboration

Figure 5.1 A mindful art therapy session. Source: The author

Figure 5.1 describes a process approach to a mindful art therapy session. Although these are set out as phases, the process is reflexive, much like the colors of a quilt weaving its way across and through the whole work to capture the iterative (circular) and multidimensional nature of therapy. The phases are described as follows:

Phase one—facilitating mental openness

Facilitating mental openness through meditative mindfulness is a core feature of the process that initiates mind–body relaxation and enhances focus. That does not imply that clients in art therapy do not achieve this. However, beginning the process with focused breathing cannot be overstated for its calming effects and power to interrupt persistent anxiety, rumination, or emotional triggers that threaten to overwhelm. When your breathing slows, it signals to the body (neurochemically) that things are okay (Hanson, 2009). Most spiritual traditions have used focused breathing techniques for centuries to help people regain composure. Neuropsychologists today are finding that focusing on the breath helps to bring an overactive fight or flight response to its natural resting state and reduce stress (Hanson, 2009). Breath work and body scans (guided meditations focusing on relaxing body parts sequentially) are quick and easy ways to calm the mind and body and ground clients in sensory feelings that help them refocus and become present. There are endless meditative protocols available in book or music shops or through the internet, or you may want to produce your own.

Guided imagery has been used throughout time for healing people. Nowadays, it is increasingly valued by helping professionals to reduce anxiety and pain symptoms. Initially introduced within behaviorist psychology for flooding or extinguishing fears, panic or trauma, guided meditations now tend to be less structured within remedial protocols and are more about creating an open space for imaginative metaphors. Listeners may be carried off to far-off lands, ocean beaches or walks through nature, with or without imaginary protective guides where they are free to let the mind wander and engage in reverie.

Guided imagery is particularly useful for helping clients explore painful emotions with psychological safety. But pain is pain after all, and although neither mindfulness nor art therapy will necessarily make the pain go away, they do provide a context for clients to change their relationship to pain. For example, by learning to accept and make room for emotional pain, clients will often stop struggling or trying to change things and reinvest the energy by choosing to explore pain with openness, sensitivity and compassion.

Several years ago, perhaps as an artifact of my yoga practice, I decided to incorporate background music into therapy. The idea was to deepen the meditative state and enhance visual imagery. I have found that clients visibly seem to relax to it and engage in the therapeutic tasks (art and reflection) more readily. But music is a personal thing, as is the decision of whether or not to use it.

Phase two—processing experience

Both attentional and intentional processes come into play during the art-making phase.

When a person sits quietly in meditation, the mind and body relax. During rumination, the mind wanders, but eventually settles on thoughts, feelings, attitudes or sensations (whether real or imagined) that stand out most at the time (Mikulas, 2011). In the overlap between phases one and two of the mindful art-therapy process, deeper concentration contributes to art expression through decentering.

Decentering (mental distancing) through relaxation and guided meditation can help clients gain perspective over areas of life where they feel stuck or overwhelmed. Decentering originated as a philosophical notion referring to an open mental space for play. As clients begin to detach from ordinary logic, and mentally distance themselves from emotional pain, they begin to see, perceive, and explore new ways of responding through line, shape, or color. From within this relaxed attitude, openness replaces the need to defend experience within self-imposed limits or the constraints of others.

Art expression fills an inner need and becomes a method for releasing, acknowledging, or transforming negative feelings (Betensky, 1995). Embodiment through art happens through the interplay of perceptual experience (cognitive, emotional, visual, sensory). As cognitive, emotional and visual tensions are mobilized, they personify experience and "speak" through the image (Flynn, 2004). The unconscious embodiment of art activity might be articulated in the way a client confidently or hesitantly handles the art materials, leans on their elbow and closer in towards the art work, appearing deep in thought while drawing or erasing or redrawing the image or a part of it. Or perhaps where the audible scribblings of pens, pencils or brushes signal a desire to make things right (McNiff, 2004).

Moreover, the actualizing tendency to create something provides a context for exploring emotions and taking safe risks. There are no guidelines for how a person should think, feel or draw, nor rules about whether they are right or not. As clients engage their sensibilities through art-making without fear of judgment, they also work within the boundaries of their sensitivities. As clients act on their intentions, they begin to make sense of their experience through the properties of form, line, or color.

Creative solutions can be expressed through the intentional use of color, shape, and lines, as well as the energy brought to an image; for example in the transparent qualities of color, or perhaps through strong kinesthetic momentum. The tangible and visible overlap occurs in relation to visceral and emotional tensions that can highlight anything from unresolvedness to inner resourcefulness. If an image doesn't come, we work with key thoughts, words or ideas that came up in the guided meditation. However, in most cases, an image is produced and the image becomes an anchor and signpost for guiding discussion toward meaningful memories, associations, and feelings.

Phase three—interpretation

Images provide an anchor and signpost for emotional experience. Although it's only natural to look at a client's artwork and begin to develop an idea of what it's all about, it's important to suspend (bracket) any biases. While it's best to let clients guide the interpretation of images (rather than a therapist attempting to psychologically analyze through the image), a common goal among therapists is to facilitate some level of psychotherapeutic understanding (Rubin, 2005).

Franklin and Politsky (1992) introduced a five-stage multidimensional framework for interpretation that preserves the integrity of the artwork, while enabling the artist to remain the expert in his or her world. This framework, although offered some 20 years ago, still holds sway as a guideline for art therapists and researchers. In brief, the stages refer to developing an attitude free of preconceived ideas, engaging with the visual elements of the image, attuning to the personal and cultural styles of the client, and exploring hunches. These overlap with a mindful approach by therapists in maintaining an open, non-judgmental, and curious attitude toward discovery.

In keeping with the notion of the "client as expert" and "therapist as witness" (Anderson and Goolishian, 1988), we try to make sense of what a client wants to understand. This is to better understand the attitudes and intentions underlying emotional pain that bring insight into what a client is feeling as a result. This is an important part of direct experiencing where a client is afforded the opportunity to be heard and validated, and is also given opportunities to clarify and negotiate meanings. Being understood not only enables a client to feel heard and validated, but also aids adaptive functioning. Equally vital is the capacity for therapists to work collaboratively with clients; co-constructing meaning so that the therapeutic dialogue facilitates understanding, insights, acceptance, and the processing of emotions (Linesch, 1994). This occurs largely through questioning, and cognitive attentional mindfulness skills serve well in remaining image-centered and guiding the reflexive dialogue with openness.

What actually happens in mindful art therapy?

When art and mindfulness are paired, this deepens introspection and helps people to turn toward rather than away from emotional pain with openness, novelty, and psychological safety. Choosing to observe, rather than getting caught up emotionally, enables a person to step back and watch how life is unfolding, rather than trying to control it. As we acknowledge an evershifting stream of consciousness, we feel less trapped and more open to change. In the absence of needing to defend or avoid life experience, mindful art therapy seems to serve the psychological function of locating us within current life experience with greater sensitivity and self-compassion.

In summing up the phases of the mindful art-therapy processes, we can begin to see the reflexive integrative nature. On the whole, turning inward through guided meditation and art helps people connect with deeper mental processes, beyond the worded world of talk therapy alone, or art therapy without mindfulness. In the experiential phase, I have found that most clients will draw, though some prefer to write a narrative after a guided meditation. In either case, we explore the personal meanings of what is communicated, in the interpretive phase, which often leads us back through other phases of therapy.

Interestingly, how a client attends to meditation or the art task can highlight their readiness or resistance to explore sensitive material. You can visibly see a client relax, when she or he drops their shoulders and lets go of tension or stress during breath work, or perhaps fidgets in the chair; similarly during the art task, when she or he leans closer in, in deep concentration, or muddles through the art supplies for a length of time to find just the right ones, or erases or starts again, or approaches the task with speed and confidence, or perhaps reticence. These non-verbal signals embody inner tensions and provide clues to the synergies between inner and outer mental life. Working collaboratively and exploring these clues as well as the images, generally points to the deeper emotions that fuel anxiety or depression and which keep people stuck.

PART THREE

Metaphorically Speaking

Building on previous theoretical chapters, this section introduces a series of clinical case studies to illustrate various aspects of the method. These case studies deal with anxiety and depression as the core underlying emotional states interfering with life values, goals, and aspirations. Setting out to overcome anxiety or depression can be a lofty ideal when you're not sure how you got there, or what to do about it.

In therapy, we attempt to explore what anxiety or depression feels like through mindfulness and art. Being present, aware, and curious about painful emotions can help loosen rigid styles of thinking and break down cycles of mental-health suffering. In mindfulness, there is no striving or resistance. Instead, clients turn gently toward emotional pain with detachment as they open up to it. As clients gain emotional distance, they can begin to see things for what they are (in the fullness of *all* life experience). In my experience with clients, I have found that depression and anxiety underlie most other issues and can often be worked through restoratively.

Clients often come to art therapy after having already tried conventional talk therapy. In many instances, these clients have already "said all there is to say" or want to try something different, or more spiritual. I'm often asked if art therapy is spiritual and my sense is that when we turn inward through mindfulness, we are better able to capture the spiritual essence of our authentic nature. But some may not feel that way, which is okay.

Most clients take instantly to relaxing in guided meditation as it calms them down and interrupts mind chatter. For many, the novel experience of noticing, rather than discussing or getting caught up in drama, is new for them. This seems especially true for those confronting things like fear or anger where feelings of shame or guilt can otherwise result in talking around important issues. However, in contemplative mindfulness, all things can be considered in the privacy and safety of inner stillness; there's no judgment, or need to buy in, just an awareness of inner consciousness where emotional pain can be witnessed and seen for what it is, beneath ordinary defenses or ego.

CHAPTER 6

Painting Through Depression

Clients are often prescribed homework to do between sessions. This helps consolidate skills learned in therapy, which can then be transferred to everyday life. In art therapy, homework often takes the form of art or journaling activities. In mindful art therapy, homework begins by engaging in mindful practice before the art activity to enable the two to work in concert. Facilitating relaxation and a psychologically safe mental stance toward emotion-processing is less threatening for clients who feel overwhelmed by their emotions. Not only do they find solace or respite from persistent rumination, but they also become proactive in their healing through creative processing. As mindfulness helps clients to become more present with experience, the art task provides a context for processing deeper intuitive thoughts and feelings that keep people stuck. The case study illustrated below shows how this client developed a repertoire of mindful art therapy which she used at home to explore and articulate her depression.

Bridget
Bridget, a 26-year-old woman, was referred by her general practitioner (GP) for the psychotherapeutic treatment of depression. She had been experiencing lethargy, insomnia, reduced motivation, and at times lacked lucidity. When she was introduced to therapy, she had very high distress on the Kessler Psychological Distress Scale (K-12) and her depression was confirmed as severe on the Beck Depression Inventory (BDI).

Bridget was shy, softly spoken and often looked down or away when she spoke. She saw herself as a high achiever and somewhat of a perfectionist, adding further to her stress given her current lack of energy and motivation. Bridget reasoned that she wanted to overcome her depression, yet lacked the impetus to engage in healthy eating, exercise, or her work. She often woke in the middle of the night, and although not ruminating on anything in particular, she found it difficult to get back to sleep. Beyond normal everyday stress, Bridget mentioned she was a worrier.

Despite her lack of energy, Bridget was curious about her depression and wanted to explore it. In the early stages of therapy, she began experimenting with mindful art therapy to get a better handle on her feelings. Following a brief guided meditation, she produced a faintly penciled lone pink bird across the center of the page. Although aloft, the bird had a flat, lifeless quality that lacked animation and gave the impression of being suspended in mid air. The image, entitled *Freedom*, "[was]…about wanting to be free of depression." Somewhat akin to her demeanor at the time, the still bird mirrored Bridget's persona in therapy: cognizant that she wanted to move forward, but not feeling able, or knowing how.

Figure 6.1 Jellyfish (see color plate)

In stark contrast, a more animated image appeared in the second session providing clues to Bridget's deeper emotional experience. A vivid blue jellyfish floating above a murky pond seemed to mark a kinesthetic loosening up of her inner anxiety and struggles with depression. Bridget explained: "This is a jellyfish and the stingers I feel from others…it's…probably a mixture of guilt, inadequacy, thinking less of myself…not that I'm not worthy…but my actions aren't fruitful… good enough."

As we explored this theme in subsequent sessions, a visual landscape of emotional memories associated with feelings of rejection emerged from years earlier. As simple images brought inner calm, cathartic relief and reflexive insights, Bridget began to appear less ill at ease. By the fifth session, her outward demeanor had visibly shifted from shy and reticent to open and trusting as she came to accept, rather than resist, her depression.

Bridget's visual montage of depression

In the same way that one might walk past and then return to an artwork to complete something unfinished in the psyche (Betensky, 1995), Bridget chose to explore her previous image of the jellyfish outside of therapy between the fifth and sixth sessions. Initially she googled images, settling eventually on a photo of a six to seven foot jellyfish with people swimming around it. Contemplating mindfully, she reasoned that some jellyfish were not to be feared, and if other people could swim near one without being stung, perhaps she could too. This led Bridget to explore the meaning of her earlier artwork through a series of paintings, which she brought to the following (sixth) session. Figures 6.2–6.5, undertaken between sessions, are presented in the order they were shown to me.

Image one: creative freedom

Creative freedom enables clients to take risks in art from within the inner landscape, risks that they may otherwise not take in real life (the outer landscape). The first image represented freedom from limitations that were both self-imposed and imposed by others. This marked the beginning of Bridget's freedom from perfection as well as giving herself permission to take risks, explore, and enjoy the journey.

Figure 6.2 Creative freedom (see color plate)

Bridget remarked:

> I was thinking about the jellyfish from earlier (session 2). I
> started with the dark ones...but there were some positive
> qualities...they were not as daunting as I thought...there was
> something light about them. It starts out disorganized then fits
> more with the style...but they were quite random at first...and
> I was mulling over the tumultuous thoughts...painting them
> out. Normally I'd draw and worry about getting it right...this
> was free...I played with it till I got something I like. After
> I did that I produced things I like. I was experimenting and
> instinctive...more spontaneous and less contrived.

This is about breaking the cycle of rigid thinking. In allowing herself
creative freedom, Bridget was able to detach instinctively from self-
imposed perfectionism.

Image two: symbolic color

Betensky (1995) has suggested that color has both a structure
and therapeutic function in its relationship to the emotional self.
Spontaneous images emerge like a stream of thought to further
unravel deeper urges that underlie emotion experience. Here,
mindfulness skills helped Bridget to turn safely toward, rather than

shy away from or internalize her fear from a safe mental distance. Through mindfulness she was able to be open to it, and through art she was able to express visually and explore its deeper resonance.

Figure 6.3 Symbolic color (see color plate)

Bridget remarked:

> The second one evolved from the first because I started with blue...accepting that the jellyfish might be more appealing... with a good quality...instead of scary or frightening. I liked blue because it was calming...and reminded me that everything was alright...happy as opposed to a dishwater grey or murky brown (washed out and confusing).

The resourceful use of prized colors such as blue for calming further enabled Bridget to entertain other perspectives about the jellyfish; that it was not as frightening or confusing as originally thought, and that there could be positive attributes in exploring her fears.

Image three: psychological flexibility

Carl Rogers has reminded us that people learn to tolerate ambiguity when they come to see that "all trees are not green" (1961, p.114). Tolerating ambiguity involves taking risks. Taking risks is a hallmark of art therapy where trees can be purple, yellow, red, blue, and so on without appearing wrong. The capacity to confront problems from a different perspective through art helps to free up rigid thinking while mindfulness encourages acceptance in seeing things as they are. This contributes to psychological flexibility.

Figure 6.4 Psychological flexibility (see color plate)

Bridget remarked:

> The third evolved from the second into green. They were different but all right with themselves. Previously I would have dismissed green...but experimenting with this I found something interesting...I liked it [green] but never used it... when I used green and brown I was saying I can make what I want...I don't have to use other colors if I want to be different.

Here, the idea of positive color choices assisted Bridget in entertaining the idea of self-acceptance. Furthermore, her resourceful use of green enabled her to free herself from the expectations of others in order to feel all right about being different.

Image four: creative solutions

Mindfulness helps a person connect with inner divisions and unresolvedness. As an idea germinates, as with Bridget's jellyfish image in session two, creative resolutions can sometimes come full circle. This was the last image Bridget showed me, yet the first she articulated that brought her to this point.

Figure 6.5 Creative solutions (see color plate)

This one was like a picture I found on the internet...it was the size of a person...six to seven feet long. It's different to the others...the textures, hues, and tentacles. But scary to think it's in the ocean. I found it quite disturbing...intriguing...looking at the dimensions. It looks scary but people were swimming around it...just swimming!

I did this [artwork] because it needed to be more visible... there was a lot to it...different little bits...and so I kept painting the colors...and it was useful thinking about the different aspects that make it up...the colors and textures. Because again it's not something I would usually paint or draw...so it's quite different. And I accepted it and saw something interesting in things I would have dismissed.

By this stage, color had become a mindful source of visual language for Bridget through which she could confront the fear and confusion that were contributing to her depression and keeping her stuck. Here, mindfulness enhanced her ability to seek creative solutions.

Summing up

In this chapter, the emphasis has been on how mindfulness combines with direct emotional experiencing through art. The capacities to intuit and directly experience through art are phenomenological concepts that describe perceiving through the senses and mind (Betensky, 1995). Mindful art therapy can deepen the inward turn and facilitate this journey. For Bridget, the skills of mindfulness enabled her to accept and explore rather than give in to her depression, whereas using art to problem-solve seemed to provide her with a kind of "mental-health tool box" for mindful art therapy for accessing, perceiving, and processing her fears.

This case study illustrates Bridget's capacity for resilience by exploring the emotional resonance of her depression and allowing herself creative freedom, experimentation with symbolic color, and psychological flexibility. Within three months, her BDI depression level had lowered to within the normal range, and it remained so six months later. While she has since reported an occasional depressive episode, Bridget has learned to accept and normalize her emotions and to resolve everyday ups and downs both mindfully and creatively.

Reflecting on the journey is important to gain a better understanding of how past, present, and future horizons meld and impact on life. As Bridget became more familiar with the skills of mindfulness, she confronted her depression through the freedom of art by spontaneously producing a visual montage of emotional experience. Using color as a resource, she teased out various facets of the jellyfish stingers (fear), so that each artwork took on a role of its own; integrated but separate from the one before it. Reflecting retrospectively, Bridget was able to confront safely deeper feelings that were previously inaccessible and difficult to harness in words. Essentially, mindful art therapy opened Bridget to deeper associations about her depression, where, in "mulling over the tumultuous thoughts…[she was] painting them out."

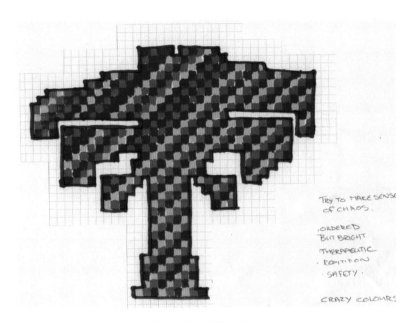

Figure 4.1 Sally 1: Trees

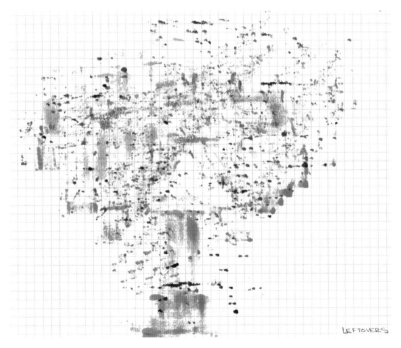

Figure 4.2 Sally 2: Trees

Figure 6.2 Creative freedom

Figure 6.3 Symbolic color

Figure 6.4 Psychological flexibility

Figure 6.5 Creative solutions

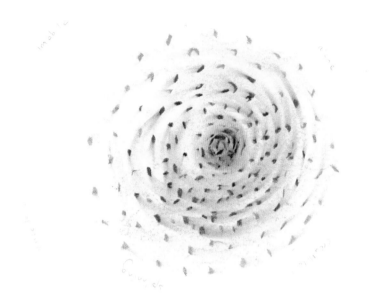

Figure 10.1 'Contemplating panic'

Figure 10.2 Looking at panic from familiar places

Figure 10.4 Panic floating away

Figure 10.5 The dissolve

Figure 12.1 The old burnt-out car

Figure 14.1 Feeling trapped/cage

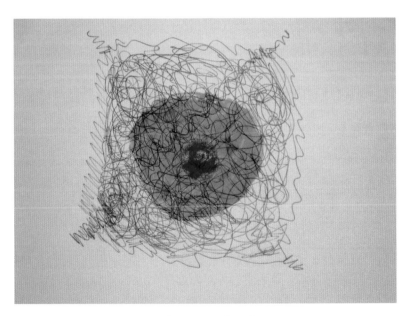

Figure 14.2 Dread

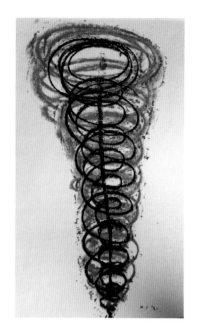

Figure 16.1 Chaos

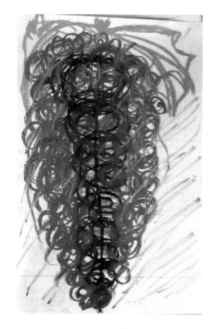

Figure 16.2 Grapes

CHAPTER 7

Good Grief

When a first pregnancy is welcomed by parents, the mind and body become fully engaged. Beyond the physiological and perhaps lifestyle changes of women, the hearts and minds of potential parents become wrapped up in fantasies of caring for a baby, searching for baby clothes and furniture, or imagining taking their child to the zoo or on other fun outings. Pragmatic considerations such as whether a woman will continue working after the child is born, financial planning, and planning the baby's room are also often thought out.

Unexpected pregnancy loss, however, can result in disenfranchised grief, loss of knowing what to do next, or how to carry on. Even in light of the support of well-meaning others, a woman and her partner are faced with negotiating grief and loss.

Morgan and Asher

I first met Morgan and her husband Asher in the hospital. Morgan had just given birth to stillborn twins. The couple were in shock and disbelief following a traumatic series of events owing to twin-to-twin transfusion syndrome (TTTS). TTTS is common in up to 90 percent of women carrying identical twins who share a single placenta. Loss of one or both twins is common in up to 90 percent of women expecting identical twins if TTTS occurs prior to 24 weeks' gestation. In one third of cases, when one baby is lost, the other will also be lost.[11]

Emotionally vulnerable and physically weak, Morgan and Asher shared what happened in a series of events leading up to the birth. First, Morgan underwent surgery in the hope of correcting the TTTS. However, the smaller of the twins failed to thrive. Then, in the hope of saving the larger twin, Morgan required a second emergency surgical

---

1 See http://www.tttsfoundation.org for more information.

procedure. However, the second twin died and Morgan simultaneously fell seriously ill. A week later, Morgan gave birth to stillborn twins.

Although Morgan and Asher understood the situation, it was devastating to come to terms with. Trying to make any sense of it seemed futile and the efforts of well-meaning others brought little solace. Asher was at a loss of how to *be* with Morgan, and Morgan was experiencing the raw pain and disconnect between her mind and body that seemed to be crying out: "You've given birth, now where are your babies?" As her emotions deteriorated, Morgan felt she was moving "numbly on a journey without a road map." Adding to their confusion were feelings of disenfranchised love and awe for their twins who they would never get to know. Morgan and Asher left the hospital filled with grief as their dreams of parenthood were shattered and replaced by the need to plan a funeral.

A breath at a time, a step at a time…

In the early sessions, I introduced mindfulness skills and particularly breath work to calm Morgan and Asher's anxiety and help them begin to come to terms with the traumatic events in their lives. Breath work provided Morgan with a skill for calming an acute, overactive stress reaction to post-pregnancy hormones, as well as the loss. Our mantra for therapy became "one breath at a time, one step at a time," and this set the stage for working toward a psychologically safe space in which to allow painful emotions to surface and be explored, expressed, and unpacked through art. The process was slow, moving at a pace that enabled Morgan to gradually come to terms with what had happened. On several occasions we just sat quietly together, Morgan, Asher and I, or just Morgan and I. There were several instances where, midway through her story, she stopped to take a few deep breaths to gain composure.

Early artworks

Morgan's early artworks attest to a range of shock, panic, anger, and grief. But a short while later, these early drawings became almost transparent, faint in line and color, echoing the multifaceted feelings of disconnect that resulted from the stillbirth (loss of the babies, her identity as an expectant mother, knowing how to *be* in the world). Despite many supportive family members and friends, Morgan chose to distance herself, particularly as a number of her friends were expecting, including one who was pregnant with twins. By keeping with the slow and open pace of mindfulness, Morgan was able to just *be* present with whichever emotion she was swept up in at the time. With mindful attunement, we met each one, turning gently toward the emotion with breathing and guided meditation as our entry point to explore it further.

Along the road of awareness

As the grief process gradually began to unfold over the next few months, Morgan explained: "It's like more layers of shock peeling away…[in] a problem that can't be solved." She missed being pregnant as well as the anticipation of motherhood, and her artworks during this period were more organic, symbolizing various phases of pregnancy that she had been forced to bid farewell to. These works pertaining to herself were mingled with others highlighting Morgan's ever present awareness of her friends' advancing pregnancies. This was taking its toll on her, yet all the while Morgan never lost hope that she would fall pregnant again.

Over time, Morgan began to build her strength and functioning reasonably well by eating healthy food, exercising, and cultivating a mindful relaxation practice. At this point, she began to connect with a handful of close friends, though saying "When I leave them, I still go home to what happened." She was never able to escape it, and as feelings of numbness gradually gave way to anger and feelings of betrayal, there was a shift in her style of art, which went from faint transparencies to bold, bellowing kinesthetic images. The verbal descriptions that accompanied these images were equally intense, highlighting the mind–body connection through her capacity to express her anger both visually and verbally through the method. Although the intensity of Morgan's anger subsided at times, it remained like an undercurrent and would crescendo from time to time.

Morgan announced one day that the hospital auxiliary group had given her a box with "a lot of memorabilia" at the time of the stillbirth; knitted outfits, hats, photos, teddy bears, and the like. Although Morgan seemed on the one hand to want to search for it, she wasn't ready. And even if she did find the box, she wasn't quite sure what to do with it, now that the girls were gone. We agreed that if Morgan did find the box and wanted to bring it or any of the items to therapy, she was welcome to do so.

However, a few weeks later Morgan announced with a mixture of excitement and trepidation that she was pregnant again. When we began to explore what a healthy pregnancy might look like, Morgan was drawn back to the twins and felt torn between the two pregnancies. Although Morgan and Asher were delighted about the new pregnancy, Morgan did not want to become dismissive and "forget the girls," nor did she want to announce her pregnancy to others in case something went wrong or "they might forget the girls, or what happened." In light of her ambivalence, it was essential to devote time to both aspects, and so this phase of therapy was focused mindfully and artfully in part on remembrance of the girls and in part on assisting Morgan to be present with her current pregnancy.

In remembrance of the girls

Figure 7.1 Collage

A few weeks after announcing her pregnancy, Morgan arrived with a large plastic box filled with memorabilia for the twins. As Morgan fished through an assortment of footprints on paper, teddy bears and the like, she pulled out two outfits, one for each of the girls. As she did so, we lay them side by side in a collage of sorts, giving Morgan the opportunity to speak about each of the girls separately. When she was finished, Morgan produced a photograph of herself and Asher, holding the twins. This seemed to be the most confronting, but as she placed the photo behind the outfits, it was almost as though the whole picture became complete. Even so, there was a pivotal moment where Morgan seemed less hijacked by her emotions and more able just to talk about them. The collage seemed to dissolve anger and despair, and suspend us in the presence and fullness of the crisis as Morgan shared the details of it in greater depth than before. She recalled moments of joy in her retelling of giving birth, followed by the shock and heartbreak of the twins' deaths. She also recalled what others said and did, their concern for Morgan's health, and the heart-rending aftermath of the funeral.

Changing tides

As remnants of grief mingled with a semblance of peace for the twins, Morgan found her way back to her advancing pregnancy, and the prospect of a healthy pregnancy and motherhood. But this was not to be; despite an apparently healthy pregnancy, and for unexplained medical reasons, Morgan gave birth to another stillborn baby girl. The shock and disbelief sent Morgan and Asher back to the raw grief that was already too familiar to them. Another stillbirth, another funeral: when I visited them in hospital, they were both operating from a state of survival and coping.

When Morgan returned to therapy, her anguish was palpable. She said she was "just surviving. It all feels like part of a single experience [the loss of the twins, the loss of the recent baby]…it's all too familiar…like a recurring nightmare…it's like the new grief is eclipsing the inner peace that I began to feel for the twins." In an effort to sort things out in her mind, she announced that she needed cognitive behavioral therapy (CBT). However, in keeping with our therapeutic approach to take things "a breath at a time, a step at a time," we began with a short period of guided relaxation, in which Morgan could stop and draw at any point in time if she chose to do so. We used this process for approximately ten minutes, in which Morgan went from moments of calm to audible bursts of magic marker on paper that culminated in 25 words strewn randomly across the page.

Figure 7.2 Words on the page

As we worked through the words that stood out most to Morgan, she began to see how her anguish and resilience were competing for headspace. Morgan reflected:

> I recognize the negative self-speak now…and how I begin to spiral downwards…I saw it yesterday…I recognized the difference. Then I had to rebuild myself with things like, "you are worth it…you need to drop the fear and anger." I was trying to pull myself out of it with positive self-talk.

But having already tried to make sense logically of traumatic events in her mind, Morgan found CBT ineffective in helping her change how she felt. Even in light of these conventional attempts to bolster resilience logically through positive self-talk, fear and anger continued to bubble under the surface. As such, we moved on to an ACT protocol, which Morgan was already familiar with. This was not going to make her fear and anger go away, but it provided Morgan with an opportunity to change her relationship to her feelings. Using the ACT hexaflex (Harris, 2009), we found a mindful way forward to address the reality gap (Harris, 2012) without Morgan feeling bogged down by painful thoughts or emotions. We continued with this protocol for the next few months.

Summing up

Understanding the importance of Morgan's readiness to confront emotional pain necessitated moving through therapy "a breath at a time, a step at a time." This is not to say that we do not attempt to do this with all clients, but the phrase has been repeated throughout the case study to illustrate that in the face of repeated trauma, there was a need to proceed slowly and compassionately to avoid being swept up by the drama.

In Morgan and Asher's case, emotional trauma continued to unfold throughout the course of therapy. In light of this, it was necessary to shape therapy as we proceeded in order to maintain a psychologically safe environment in which Morgan could allow for her emotional frailty. With the mindfulness tools of breathing and guided meditations providing a calm entry point in which to explore painful emotions openly, compassionately and non-judgmentally (Hanh, 1999), art provided opportunities to shape experience (Levine, 2005), and mindfully appraise it with compassion (Kashdin and Ciarrochi, 2013). As difficult as it was for Morgan not to get emotionally hijacked by her feelings, she cultivated a daily mindfulness practice outside of therapy. She listened regularly to guided meditations or apps for relaxation, and she introduced them as best she could in real time, when caught up in the reactive phase of her emotions.

Reflecting on the trajectory of her art tasks, we can see how the nature of Morgan's emotions directly related to how and what she drew, wrote or created in the fullness and immediacy of moment. In the vein of needing to "shift gears" (Wadeson, 1987) with appropriate therapeutic art tasks, we were able to meet the traumatic burdens of shock and anguish along the way. In addition, because emotional memory functions well in helping clients shape their experience through art (Levine, 2005), both contemplative and cognitive mindfulness methods helped to facilitate the inward focus and remain open in the reflexive dialogue. Furthermore, the interface of creating a therapeutic space of psychological safety proved to be a significant element in shaping therapy through the core conditions of empathy, congruence, and positive regard.

Whereas drawing initially provided Morgan with a cathartic release for overwhelming emotions, it also brought order to chaos through form, color, and shape in her artworks (McNiff, 2004). Metaphorically, these were played out in transparent images when feeling "lost," and bold visual outbursts when experiencing intense periods of anger. As constructions of re-experiencing what she was feeling at the time, the tangible nature of these images enabled Morgan to stop and reflect, even if only momentarily, on the course of her grief.

The immediacy and openness of writing out her thoughts after the second stillbirth served a similar purpose in helping Morgan authentically confront both her emotional frailties and inner strengths (Pennebaker, 2004). In keeping with Morgan's propensity to "think things through" however, the CBT protocol fell short in helping her appraise the emotional memories that vied for her attention. But in this instance, the ability to reflect on her cognitions, emotions, perceptions, and sensations simultaneously (metacognition) through mindfulness (Kashdin and Ciarrochi, 2013) enabled Morgan to contextualize the crises within her resilience and hope.

The rich, corrective experience of the memorabilia collage added a further layer of integrative power to both the existence and the loss of the twins. It was during this art task that Morgan could begin to address the mind and body disconnect she had been grappling with (Frost, 2010). The box in some ways seemed to mirror the womb, and served as a tangible context for beginning to make peace with what happened.

On the whole, mindful art therapy provided Morgan with an anchor and signpost for *being* with the unpredictable nature of her trauma and grief. As a therapist, it was a privilege to provide a safe psychological space and, in keeping with the sentiments of Coryell (2007), "It is…a great honour to sit with people and share the burden of grief we all must carry at certain moments of our lives and so often alone (p.108)." Morgan chose to have her case study shared here in the hope that it would guide therapists or other parents of stillborn children, and perhaps help normalize their experience.

Morgan has since given birth to a healthy baby boy.

CHAPTER 8

Voice of Reason

Early on in my psychology career, a supervisor explained anger as the flip side of depression. This was her educated hunch, based on several decades of experience. It has led me to ponder the idea ever since. Anger is a normal human emotion, which, if managed properly, seldom leads to any harm. In times of need, it serves to defend oneself or prevent oneself from being taken advantage of. Being angry is one experience—being an angry person, quite another. When anger is suppressed, it can bubble under the surface and contribute to an ongoing narrative that drives behavior.

Although coherent narratives help us make sense of our lives (Kashdin and Ciarrochi), they can also keep us stuck. As one learns to encounter the narrative mindfully, the shift from striving to "make things right," to accepting "how things are," can be freeing. While it is sometimes difficult for clients to confront strong emotions head on, mindful art therapy offers mental distance to explore the personal narrative in a non-threatening way. Gaining mental distance also enables a client to separate him- or herself from the conceptual meaning of emotions such as anger, and grasp its deeper meaning. Furthermore, in contrast to logically reasoning through it, mindful reflection on artworks can help a client to reappraise their life story and begin to change their relationship to it.

Max

Max, a 30-year-old male, came to therapy to explore his depression and anger. In the typically stoic manner in which he was raised, tears were there but difficult to access. Having recently and unexpectedly lost his mother, sadness gave way to an enduring sense of depression that he said had begun several years earlier. At the time, feelings of regret for not having been kinder to his mother were brewing under the surface. As we worked mindfully through the grieving process, Max began to acknowledge his difficulty connecting with emotions, and particularly in managing his anger.

Anger was something Max had *experienced* all of his life in various ways of lashing out. Beyond classic sparks of embodied anger that resulted in flying off the handle, yelling, and fistfights, Max reflected that rage seemed be common in the males in his family. For example, he recalled how his father used to go out in the shed and bang things around when he was angry, or when he himself yelled at others. He also recollected how his six-year-old nephew, who despite minimal contact with Max or his father, flew into fits of rage (balling his fists, narrowing his eyes, silently fuming) when he didn't get his own way. Whereas these insights might previously have spurred helplessness, ambivalence or resignation, reflecting on the temperamental nature of males in his family helped Max take it in without judging it.

A trajectory through anger

We initially set up an "anger diary" to gauge how and when Max expressed anger, as well as observe what anger felt like, and how it was affecting his life and relationships. Interestingly, the more Max began to explore his anger mindfully, the more he began to turn toward it, rather than trying to avoid it. In response to a mix of frustration and grief, he penciled a small brick in the lower left side of the paper and listed "what's blocking him" (anger, fear, panic, orderliness, and grief). In the next session, he mentioned that "Anger is a by-product of panic. I don't know the words but feels like there's no progress forward…time passes but I'm getting nowhere." To this he produced an image of his raw anger in the guise of a bomb, with a fuse that was about to go off.

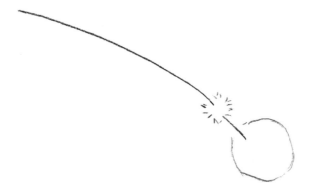

Figure 8.1 Anger fuse

Penciled simply, the bomb—like Max—had an explosive fuse that triggers easily. The smudges around the image were in terms of a lifetime of deep-seated feelings that he found difficult to verbalize and cope with. Reflecting further led Max to reconsider his anger as a signal for destructive behavior that he was beginning to understand as a shield for feelings of low self-worth.

As he continued to familiarize himself with the mindful art-therapy method, Max felt more at ease exploring emotions that were previously hidden, and experienced as frustration or projected through anger. He did this in the quiet space of guided meditations, where logic gave way to detached mental openness and simple drawings witnessed to the personal narrative he had constructed for himself.

One day, describing how he felt alone and separate from his friends, Max mentioned that "he knows he's where he wants to be… but feels alone there." However, his quest to "better himself" and individuate himself from family and childhood friends resulted in a somewhat perfectionist attitude about the "way things should be" that left nothing to chance. This rigid style of thinking gradually loosened up through guided meditations and a progression of drawings where Max came to accept, rather than trying to control life around him.

As time went on, Max recognized that he was not powerless and could develop strategies to manage his anger more adaptively. In another session, Max drew a line demarcating the things he could control (listed above the line) and things he couldn't (listed below the line). Reflecting on this image (not shown here) led Max to accept and take responsibility for his own power. This marked a pivotal point where Max began to redirect his energy toward important life decisions to do with career and study choices, as well as the way he wanted to be in his relationships. As it happened, this session was timely as work stress had begun to escalate over previous weeks, which forced Max to make decisions about his career path. In tandem with cultivating a mindful art-therapy practice, Max constructed what he referred to as an *Anger Commonplace Book*.

Figure 8.2 "Anger commonplace book"

The idea of a "commonplace book" originated from early European scholars who recorded information in books much like scrapbooks. Taking this further, Max paired the idea with a modern diary where he could record his awareness of his anger, as well as poignant moments of calm. This was empowering, not only in taking the courage to look directly at his anger and his capacity to manage it, but also in spurring him on to develop self-directed mindfulness mantras that he could use in real time.

Summing up

Over a lifetime of suppressing his emotions verbally, Max had never learned how to communicate anger constructively. Moreover, within a rising surge of frustration, his anger became destructive. In the shift between thinking (logically) and sensing (feeling), Max was able to move from imbuing his anger with judgment to acknowledging and experiencing its felt presence. For example, by distancing himself from it in mindfulness, he was able to identify less with it, and begin to acknowledge its presence without being consumed by it. The shift from thinking to feeling also helped Max to see anger with greater psychological flexibility and to begin to change his relationship to it. This change in perception enabled him to recognize that "the problem was his own tendency toward anger, rather than external anger-provoking people or situations" (Bien, 2006, p.194). Furthermore, the method provided Max with opportunities to develop self-compassion and connect with several positive life experiences to buttress his self-worth.

Moving out of our intellect and into our emotions through art and narratives contributes to healing (Rogers, 1993). For Max, the *Anger Commonplace Book* visually and narratively helped to mobilize his intentions for regulating anger adaptively. The more he detached himself from being an angry person to accepting himself as a person experiencing anger, the more often he found ways to normalize and safely diffuse it. By detaching from his anger, Max literally and figuratively drew it out.

CHAPTER 9

Silence Is Golden

Individuation is a process of psychological development and integration that marks when a person begins to gain autonomy from family or the collective group (Jung, 1960, 1964). As Landgarten (1975) has noted, art therapy is not only an integrative experience, it is also a pictorial journal that can be recorded and reviewed in the future, but the tangible and visible overlap reflects a person's struggle for individuation. This developmental stage can often be fraught with social anxiety where, for some, the experience is confusing, frustrating, and filled with shame. This kind of shame generally refers to a belief in one's inadequacy (Potter-Efron and Potter-Efron, 1989).

When people are socially anxious, they lose the mastery or the capacity to engage with others, particularly for those who find it difficult to pinpoint the source of their anxiety. With increased mindful awareness comes the ability to confront social anxiety with psychological safety and work toward autonomy and competence. The case study illustrated below shows how calming through mindfulness aided this client's capacity to speak through his images.

Vincent

Vincent, a 19-year-old university student, was referred by his GP for generalized and social anxiety. Having been raised in a close-knit family, Vincent grew up knowing most of the people he currently conversed with. Although he wanted to "branch out and meet new people, to learn from them," he was painfully shy and didn't know what to say or how to strike up a conversation. In light of his anxiety, it was not surprising that Vincent was reticent in therapy, often looking down or away while talking to me and role plays were initially too confrontational. Like many young people, Vincent enjoyed listening to music, although he preferred techno music without words.

Speaking of social anxiety

Vincent took easily to the guided meditations where his anxious demeanor visibly shifted to a calm, relaxed state. Despite that, he often struggled with "what to draw," and his earlier images consistently characterized his goals for therapy: a fan or a calm wind to "blow anxiety away;" a small bunny that he said stood out most because it "could speak for itself," and so on. As Vincent continued to attune to the process, he gradually found a visual voice that he could emote through.

In the eighth session, Vincent drew a prominent red stop sign on the corner of two intersecting roads that he said represented "shame." This was the beginning of naming and leaning closer in to the underlying feelings that were tied to his frustration of wanting, but not knowing how, to converse with people he didn't already know (friends of his friends, fellow students, lecturers). Shame here seemed to represent more a lack of mastery rather than personal dejection. In the tenth session, he embodied the nature of this struggle more succinctly as shown below in the image of a tightly closed clamshell (Figure 9.1), which Vincent described as "empty... with nothing to say." The strong kinesthetic fervor of bold, sketchy lines underscored by the word "empty" further emphasized the angst of feeling verbally stifled.

Getting this image out into the open seemed to deepen Vincent's understanding of his demise, bringing insights, hope, and a way forward through both visual and verbal expression. Firstly, by recognizing how "feeling empty with nothing to say" was not just "nothing," but rather a direct experience of his inability to be independent. Recognizing this then led to the construction of a rating scale illustrating the kinds of conversations Vincent wanted to have which he rated from the highest to lowest in anxiety. For example, "talking with a friend's friend was a four; talking to his university lecturer was a seven; and speaking in a job interview was a ten."

Figure 9.1 Clamshell

In a second spontaneous image following this one, Vincent drew a green "go" sign positioned along a grass-lined brick pathway. In sharp contrast to his earlier red stop sign (two sessions earlier), the go sign represented a choice and the possibility of moving on. Vincent reasoned that conversing with new people is "awkward, but I can at least find out something interesting for later use." This was his current goal for therapy, which despite social awkwardness was something he was determined and hoped to master.

Feeling more comfortable with the therapeutic process by now, we engaged in role-play using *The Art of Conversation* cards (Lamb and Howland, 1995) to rehearse various ways of approaching and navigating conversation. Over the next few weeks, Vincent continued to document what he perceived as "successful conversations" on his rating scale, and he also colored in a brick leading up to the go sign for each positive encounter. A few weeks later, and in light of these therapeutic gains, Vincent returned again to the go image, this time adding a doorway. He explained that "each time I have a conversation, it's like going through another door."

Summing up

The cliché "silence is golden" features prominently in this case study, where mental distance afforded by reverie facilitated opportunities for Vincent to establish links between heart and head. Through the method, "tuning out" meant "tuning in" to deeper levels of awareness and a much-needed voice that resulted in therapeutic gains.

The accessibility of the method enabled Vincent to speak figuratively and narratively about his social anxiety. As he struggled with autonomy and his desire to branch out and meet new people, he used mindfulness to anchor to and confront his deeper feelings, and he used art to express visually how he felt about it. Through the method, he was able to delineate his own path (literally and metaphorically) using the same visual language to move from feeling stuck (stop sign; clamshell) to gaining self-empowerment (go sign; doorway). Moreover, despite his inability to verbalize what he was feeling, visual metaphors enabled him to dialogue with his emotions and access a much-needed voice that he felt he was lacking.

The capacity to reappraise life experience mindfully can help clients break through anxiety (Kashdin and Ciarrochi, 2013), where in the absence of words, art can serve to help people speak through images (Flynn, 2004). At this deeper level, Vincent was able to re-experience, symbolize, and communicate "wanting to converse... not knowing what to say" through art. This reflects the power of mindfulness in helping him turn toward his social anxiety, and art in moving him beyond feeling stuck (Kramer, 1981; Rubin, 1984), for example, in how "feeling empty...nothing to say" found a voice in the visual image of the clamshell. Furthermore, speaking through art provided Vincent with opportunities to express feelings of shame with minimal guilt and greater acceptance (Knill *et al.*, 2005; Kramer, 1987).

Learning to listen and speak from a place of silence through mindful-based art endeavors has important implications. Vincent embodied in visual language what he initially couldn't say in words. As he continued to symbolize inner conflict (social anxiety, wanting to speak for himself, shame), he began to feel less helpless. Gradually, the shift from feeling stuck, to feeling more empowered, led us to develop tasks for conversing with others that were consistent with Vincent's desire for autonomy. As he continued to reclaim his voice mindfully and artistically, Vincent's progress became a "pictorial journey" (Landgarten, 1975) of therapeutic gains.

CHAPTER 10

Contemplating Panic

In a recent report on Mental Health (ABS, 2012a), 3 million Australians (13.6%) reported suffering from a mental or behavioral condition. Mood (affective) problems were most widely reported with depression (9.7%) and anxiety (3.8%) accounting for the most prevalent concerns. The burden of psychological disability owing to depression and anxiety has compromised daily functioning in 42 percent of adult Australians, with severe limitations reported by a further 19.8 percent (ABS, 2012b).

Depression and anxiety are common in both adults and young people. The prevalence of comorbidity is common, and if left unchecked, leads to a greater likelihood of more enduring forms of pathology (Hirschfeld, 2001). Panic for example is an extreme form of anxiety. Panic might be described as nervous tension that results in avoidance or escalates into enduring feelings of dread. Panic attacks are characterized by an acute onset of fear and apprehension. Sensing danger, the brain initiates a "fight or flight" survival response (ABS, 2008).

When panic is triggered, both mind and body are affected, producing a constellation of symptoms that may include sweating, chest pain, shortness of breath, tachycardia, trembling or faintness. Although the attack may last only for minutes, recovery time varies and can manifest itself in residual anticipatory anxiety. Panic is often treated with cognitive behavioral therapy, and in some cases medication. In recent years the Anxiety Panic Hub (Australia) has initiated a proactive approach to treatment and recovery using mindfulness strategies and art therapy (Anxiety Panic Hub, 2010).

Sophia[1]

Sophia is a 26-year-old Australian woman of Italian descent. She came to therapy with anxiety and complained of panic attacks that triggered unexpectedly and immobilized her with shortness of breath, tachycardia, and feelings of dread. Sophia mentioned feeling panicked and depressed since her mid teens. At the age of 16, she was treated with Zoloft for depression; however, as her panic was dismissed under the rubric of normal adolescence, her anxiety symptoms were left untreated. Still on Zoloft at the age of 17, Sophia felt "hopeless... and numb...[as though] life was not worth living." In a failed suicide attempt, her family responded with cultural foreboding rather than emotional support, which left Sophia feeling guilty, confused, angry, and frustrated. Over the next 18 months, Sophia suffered the loss of five family members and peers. Owing to her youth, and perhaps emotional vulnerability, Sophia's family shielded her from participating in grief rituals beyond respectful involvement. Gradually, the guilt she experienced from her own suicide attempt meshed with her unresolved grief and her depression spiraled downward. Succumbing to substance abuse and uncharacteristic angry outbursts, she eventually alienated herself from family and friends, surfacing only for work or study. The following year, Sophia travelled to Italy on a working holiday. Alongside numerous pleasant experiences, sporadic episodes of panic and depression reappeared without warning. At times she experienced nightmares, and although the dreams never quite made logical sense, the paralyzing fear often remained for days. Taking solace in the listening ear of selective acquaintances, Sophia managed her symptoms as best she could. When Sophia returned to Melbourne, she sought conventional psychotherapy.

Sophia enquired about art therapy, explaining that she felt immobilized by panic. She further expressed that the mere thought of discussing panic with someone—anyone—triggered her symptoms. As such, our early sessions were focused on familiarizing her with the mindful art-therapy process to facilitate a calm, open mindset for confronting emotions through art. Shortly after, we moved on to the task of processing anger and grief, associated with some of her earlier life experiences. As Sophia gained insights, resolve, and inner

---

1 This case study is reprinted with permission from Davis, B. (2011). "Contemplating panic: A case study in mindful art therapy." *Journal of Integrative Medicine, 16 (2)*, 22–26.

resourcefulness through the process, she came to trust it more. Gradually, we entertained the idea of "contemplating panic." This aspect of therapy is presented here as a case study and illustrates our work across five sessions of art therapy followed by a reflexive session on the body of works produced.

Session one

Having disembarked from a tram two blocks away, Sophia walked to the session in the searing summer heat. She felt exhausted when she arrived, and instantly relaxed with the guided meditation. What seems to stand out most is how the lowering of defenses facilitated the inward turn beyond Sophia's normal level of resistance to her panic. Here, she was willing and able to explore panic for the first time in over ten years. As she took to the task, the sounds of articulating the dots suggested her intention to bring it finally out in the open, whereas the kinesthetic fervor of her work seemed to imply an urgency to release it.

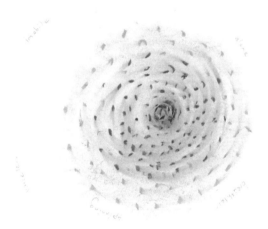

Figure 10.1 Contemplating panic (see color plate)

- Sophia: "This is the physical and emotional symptoms...what I thought I felt. It was after a deep relaxation when I power-walked to the session and listened to the guided meditation. I went deep into relaxation."

- Symbolic color: "The purple equals me. And I used the blues and turquoise because they are visually pleasing and soothing to me."

- Reflection: "Acceptance is important and that's where it all started. I wasn't going to be angry at it...just accept it."

Session two

Crossing a bridge is a common metaphor in therapy. It helps a person visualize moving from one aspect of life to another. I had not discussed bridges with Sophia, nor did I know that she feared them. However, in response to the idea of crossing one in the guided meditation, Sophia used her imagination to risk moving through her fear into new horizons. This illustrates how the process provides opportunities for clients to take risks from the safety of the therapeutic setting. Safety here means psychological safety from within the therapeutic alliance, emotional distance of mindfulness, and the freedom to explore imaginal reality.

Figure 10.2 Looking at panic from familiar places (see color plate)

- Sophia: "Crossing a bridge in the guided meditation was confrontational... because I have a fear of bridges. But I managed to cross over to a new field...an unknown place and I'm feeling freedom. What I walked away from extended beyond hills and valleys [that you see], which were already transformed. It [panic] had come from way back and transformed into freedom...the bird...and flight...it was floating."

- Symbolic color: "Most of the greens I use are like in a typical landscape. Realistic. The bird is the green-blue...it's a new color for me."

- Reflections: "This is the kind of liberation I felt from anxiety... crossing the bridge...entering a new field. It didn't have to have poppies [a previous symbol of empowerment]. Just a new field... and go there anyway...see what we make of it."

Session three

Beyond ego defenses and from within a deeper place of contemplation, clients are better able to connect with and transfer their feelings on to an artwork. Although Sophia found it difficult to talk about panic, the kinesthetic fervor of irregular pastel rings around a central "self" aided her communication of it. Using colors to modulate and safeguard her feelings further assisted her in confronting panic from a safe vantage point. Connecting with the MAT process enabled Sophia to finally bring panic out in the open.

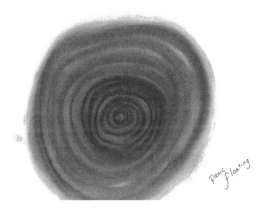

Figure 10.3 Panic floating (see color plate)

- Sophia: "This was about seeing and feeling as though it [panic] was outside of me...'in character'...'characterized.' When I see it here...it's floating outside of me. It doesn't scare me anymore."

- Symbolic color: "Purple is me. Looking at the green...it's almost a new color for me...almost a new layer of form. I think of health and vitality and growth. I think it's the same as the bird in my last drawing."

- Reflections: "That's the shifting...here [points to the central circle]. I recognize it's [panic] not on top of me. It's out where I can see it...and it's not so scary like that."

Session four

As clients become increasingly sensitive to the aesthetic resonance of their works, they come to know themselves better through their art. For Sophia, panic represented the longstanding darkness of her past, which was now beginning to shift. In continuity with her previous work, the proximal distance between self and panic in this image suggests that she may be emotionally detaching from it. Furthermore, in describing the essence of this work through its aesthetic resonance, she came to see herself separating from panic through creative empowerment.

panic floating away

Figure 10.4 Panic floating away (see color plate)

- Symbolic color: "The depth and darkness of the lower figure is a 'deep dark hole.' It doesn't feel as deep and dark as it used to...which is maybe why I put some brown in there. I am the figure floating above it...carried over from last week and I feel like the purple is me. And there's white light...and the green is me protecting myself...not protective in a defensive way...just compassionate."

- Reflections: "Here I'm realizing the negative feelings have shifted. There was something different. It didn't feel as deep...didn't feel as overwhelming…I didn't let it overwhelm me. I felt like I was rising above it."

Session five

Clients are typically taught psychological strategies that they can use outside of therapy to reduce stress. Across previous sessions, Sophia produced a number of images in which to visualize taking control over her emotions. The task for this session was to "be Zen with panic" in order to gauge present-moment awareness of it; how she was feeling now. Reflecting on a range of symbols she had produced in earlier sessions, she said: "Here I'm reflecting on tools from my [mental health] tool box." She sketched two images (not shown here): one of a dandelion to mitigate panic, and another of a quilted cape for self-compassion. She then produced a spontaneous image in which to dissolve her feelings of panic proactively.

Figure 10.5 The dissolve (see color plate)

- Sophia said: "The smudge [representing dark despair] has lightened. Using my imagination…I visualized blowing on dandelion clocks…where each tiny bit was erasing the smudge. The dandelion clocks were coming into color and erasing it."

- Symbolic color: [while looking at it upside down]: "The dandelion came into the color until color disappears. I didn't use black and brown…my intention was that [blue] representing that smudge. Brown is past negative emotions that I struggled with…the darkest despair…layers of depression…layers of anxiety and panic. They're still negative feelings…but I'm accepting and getting a handle on my anger…and I recognize sadness…and layers of grief. Panic is there as well and that's what's disappearing. The dark blue is representing the next step I'm on…going…going… gone! The negative feelings are there, but they are normal. I don't have to shut them out. I'm learning!"

- Reflection: "Here 'dissolve' was happening...like things were disappearing. I couldn't draw that and so...this [dandelion] is my favorite [tool]...it's like 'Paint' on the computer...like a shape when you are erasing it. I had a picture of myself blowing on all the dandelions...millions and millions of them...because you can only do so much with them [dandelions]...they're so small...and there are lots of bits to dissolve. I couldn't pour dandelions on them...I had to dissolve them bit by bit. On reflection that is how I got to this point...bit by bit. That goes for therapy as a whole... that [panic] was just the final hurdle."

Summing up

The case study presented here illustrates the mindful art-therapy process as a therapeutic modality rather than an adjunct to therapy. In contrast to conventional therapy where Sophia felt stifled talking about panic, she took refuge in the process, where she could look, see, discover, and confront her experience of panic beyond the worded world. Making good use of meditation and mindfulness to reduce feelings of angst, she used art resourcefully in liberating, processing and transforming her feelings of panic. From this open and accepting environment, Sophia was able to participate in her own restoration through creative empowerment.

Although the origins of her panic never came to light verbally, Sophia came to terms with it through form and color. Through her personal symbology (Landgarten, 1975), powerful images (a dandelion and blanket) helped to dissolve her panic in a compassionate rather than fearful or angry way. Through aesthetic proclivity, she used color (self=purple; soothing=turquoise; renewal=green-blue) for self-understanding and transformation. As Sophia proactively transformed her relationship to panic, her physiological symptoms gradually improved and she began to reinvest her energy in new life interests.

Looking back, Sophia reflected on the trajectory of artworks presented here, which she light-heartedly named *The Panic Collection*. She then summed up her work with me in a single Italian word:

andiamo (let's go). This she said was a metaphor for our therapy as a whole, where "panic was the final hurdle." However, this does not imply that Sophia has fully recovered from her panic; rather, it suggests that she restored her capacity to accept and deal with it through mindful art therapy.

PART FOUR

Clinical Applications in Mindful Art Therapy

CHAPTER 11

Sentient Being

We often hear about the "body's wisdom." But what does that mean? From an obvious sense, pain tells us that something is wrong. We twisted our ankle and so it now hurts. But pain can also come from emotions, for example when someone has let us down, offends us, or we think we're overweight. These experiences also hurt, and we internalize them in our minds, bodies, and emotions. We often ruminate on hurt feelings in our minds, trying to work out how to survive. But when we reason with the thinking mind, we think through our experiences or relationships, and often end up feeling unworthy or responsible in some way. Beyond the reasoning mind, these deeper feelings often seek our attention in other ways, such as anger, resignation, or withdrawal; or perhaps through things like substance abuse, overeating, or physical illness. We get stuck.

Beyond what we think, the mind is also based on what we sense and feel about the environment and ourselves. We sometimes need to surrender to these feelings in order to let inner intelligence disentangle us from deeper hurt. Sometimes we only need to meet and acknowledge what's there, at other times give voice to it. Art aids this task by providing an opportunity to express deep-felt emotions that may have been dormant for years.

Becoming aware of internalized body states allows us to know from a deeper place how stress affects our outer world, whereas art can give voice to it. These somatic markers are accessible through mindfulness and enable us to sense a connection between mind and body and their impact on thoughts, feelings, and behavior (Levine, 2010).

In mindful art therapy, as we connect with sensory experience, we come to realize that we're not the story. We allow awareness to happen through contemplation and the intentional use of form, shape, or color. We don't deny pain, but identify less with fear, guilt or anger, or the story that led us there. Dimensions of bodily consciousness, though always coursing within us, are not necessarily obvious unless we choose to bring our attention to them. But they often provide clues to connections in the mind and body and the emotional resonance of our life experience, and how or why we got there.

Emotions are the universal language of consciousness that influences how we think, feel, perceive, and behave in the world. When we distance ourselves through art and mindfulness, we can gain perspective over the things that rob us of vitality or thwart our capacity to thrive. In a therapeutic sense, it might be said that mindfulness deepens intentional awareness, whereas art gives voice to it.

Maryjane

Maryjane told me about how she got nervous whenever she had to present something at her university. Being a graduate student, there were numerous occasions when she had to do so, including meetings with her supervisor who Maryjane found intimidating. But just talking about it brought on an all too familiar nervous tic (spasm) in her neck. As her head wrenched over toward her shoulder, she winced with pain as she attempted to finish telling me about her concerns. Maryjane was overidentifying and re-experiencing what it meant to *be* anxious even though her meeting wasn't scheduled for another week, and we were sitting in the safety of the therapy session.

Following guided meditation, Maryjane sketched an image of her mother to connect with the deeper hurt she felt at the time. Although feeling guilty at having portrayed her mother in a bad light (brown and dull green "sickly" hues, "looking old, hurt and vulnerable"), Maryjane recognized that she was facing her deep-seated anger. In effect, noticing how her anxiety manifested in her body was an entry point for Maryjane's insights into exploring a difficult relationship where she felt unsupported. The effable expressions in her images gave voice to them.

Through an Acceptance and Commitment (ACT) mindfulness protocol in conjunction with her art, we continued to explore how Maryjane felt intimidated and how she internalized and expressed her anger. Being mindful brought her more closely in touch with feelings she had previously denied, which were borne out and explored through a series of images related to this key and important relationship. Several sessions later, having incorporated ACT into her daily mindset, Maryjane said that she "looks at things differently now" and that her core relationships were beginning to improve. Nor had the nervous tic reappeared, despite a recent meeting with her supervisor. Maryjane was beginning to let go of the emotional pain that fuelled her anxiety and resulted in a physical manifestation of it. As a therapeutic method, mindful art therapy thus provided an important means for Maryjane to direct her attention toward the link between her emotions and physical symptoms.

CHAPTER 12

Sense and Sensibility

We come to know the world through our "sensibilities." Sensibility is defined by the Oxford English dictionary as "the quality of being able to appreciate and respond to complex emotional or aesthetic influences; sensitivity." When we engage in mindful art therapy, we develop of sense of inner *knowing* through tacit (implied) knowledge. Much like engaging in play, mentally distancing ourselves from ordinary logic leads to a natural propensity to "be oneself" in art (Winnicott, 1971).

In the late 1990s, when I was asked to coordinate a research project using Australian indigenous art for health promotion, I learned about therapeutic art from vicarious perspectives; how iconographic images conveyed their messages of culture, health and holism beyond the worded world (Davis, 2004). In a society that draws largely on the oral tradition of storytelling, on the visual exchange of art, and on the engagement of ritual, the images needed to convey healthy lifestyle messages in the vernacular of the people they were trying to educate (Dudgeon, Garvey and Pickett, 2000).

Through this project, I began to see the parallels in Western symbolism and how conventional Judeo-Christian images similarly connected people with their identity or provided solace. The common thread seemed to be that regardless of the style of artistic symbolism, some people believed in it (Rubin, 2005). This not only brings to mind the restorative power of images (Henderson and Gladding, 1998), but also the important role of understanding a person's individual and cultural sensibilities.

Whether through vicarious or participatory art, if we want clients to engage flexibly, spontaneously, and creatively in the method, we need to get to know a bit about their personal sensibilities—a lack of mutual knowledge or shared understanding can cloud the therapeutic dialogue.

In considering how art could be used as a universal language of emotion, I began to ask clients about their cultural or religious backgrounds and their creative hobbies and interests. Making use of cultural points of view or creative activities that a person loves to do, or perhaps loved to do as a child, can engage their fundamental nature and most natural way of imaginatively exploring life. Moreover, as neuroscience has increasingly shown, mindfulness and art contribute to structural (neurological) and functional (adaptive behavior) changes. This brings to mind the significant role of combining mindfulness and art therapy. What I have found in exploring the method is that when art therapy is paired with mindfulness, it grounds a client in his or her sensibilities, where "paying attention with intention" is often more achievable.

Across my research and work with private clients, I am often reminded of the importance of working with their personal and creative sensibilities. Cheng, for example, a second-language English speaker was puzzled at first about what to draw, but he then resorted to what he *knew* and produced a calligraphic image that resonated with his background. Similarly, in a group task on self-concept, participants compared the relevance of wearing make-up in terms of cultural adornment (a Pakistani notion), being natural (the Taoist philosophy of being in harmony with nature), and using it to mask oneself (a Western perspective) (Davis, 2010). These sensibilities reflect not only how a person wants to be viewed, but also reflects the implied tacit mindset of how people feel they should be in the world.

In my experience, not everyone "knows how to draw," though most will give it a try. But if you ask clients from the outset about their hobbies or interests, you can often find a creative outlet to use therapeutically that matches their sensibilities. The following client, for example, enjoyed photography.

The extraordinary in the ordinary

These days, redundancy is a common occurrence. Both public and private industries are closing their doors or downsizing, and dismissing people who may have devoted 20, 30 or even 40 years to a company. When we hear this on the news, we may stop to think how awful it is for those workers and their families, and wonder how people will get by; what these people will do now, particularly those in their fifties. But when face to face with someone made redundant, it gives "climate change" a whole new meaning. Despite a gradually improving economy and low unemployment, redundancy and retrenchment have accounted for 3.1 percent of the working age population in Australia between 2012 and 2013 (ABS, 2014). Thousands more are at risk of losing their jobs as a result of continued cost-cutting. The emotional distress of significant loss and change as a result of unexpected events is natural. If not managed properly, people who are made redundant are at risk of depression and anxiety.

While I've had clients in the past who have seen redundancy as an opportunity for a sea change, for many, the anguish of being forced to replace an industrious working life with or without redundancy packages, the promise of exit training for new employment, or planning for retirement requires considerable psychological adjustment. In many instances, neither retirement nor skilling up for a new role was ever on the agenda, and the shock of losing an income and being let go prematurely can result in doubt, worry, and low self-worth. In addition, the lack of a daily or familiar routine and too much leisure time can be soul-destroying and result in uncertainty and a downward spiral into depression.

Ed

Ed, a man in his fifties, came to therapy having been made redundant from his job two years earlier. After 22 years in a key management role, he was unexpectedly let go. He and his wife went on a holiday immediately afterwards, which had been pre-planned and paid for long before he found out. Ed spent most of the holiday crying and clinging to his wife for emotional support. He explained that, at that time, he "found it difficult to be alone with his sadness."

Through a series of new jobs, Ed managed to remain financially solvent, subsidizing his wage with investments which enabled him to put his kids through school. However, his first job was temporary and lasted only one year. The second job was also causing him difficulty—long hours were involved, and part of his role involved letting people go when their contracts came to an end. Although the contractors often expected this, it ran against Ed's grain; it seemed to open up unresolved feelings he thought he had already dealt with. Ed remained high functioning on the surface, but his uncharacteristic moodiness and difficulty coping brought him to therapy.

Ed took to relaxation skills with ease, explaining that he had learned to "take a breath to calm down" since childhood. In the safety of mindfulness and guided meditation, he connected with the sadness he had been trying to push away for the past two years. Three rough sketches represented "a sinking feeling, that felt calmer…above the water" when he relaxed into meditation. The mental distance enabled Ed to go further into his feelings without getting caught up where, for the first time, he recognized that his "lack of motivation was actually offset by hope and light at the end of the tunnel." He further likened his mood swings to "a spirit level trying to gain balance." In this single session, Ed began to connect with deeper feelings underneath his moods, and also his capacity for resilience. Yet these inner divisions were unsettling and continued to play out in his mood swings. Although Ed seemed to appreciate processing his emotions through guided meditation, he struggled a bit with the drawing, and preferred to talk or write about them.

Before the next session, Ed wrote requesting three additional counseling sessions in which "to gather a range of skills to have at his disposal" should his moods or depression threaten to overwhelm him again. Consistent with his goals for counseling, and in response to his high level of functioning and psychological mindedness, it seemed fitting to introduce cognitive attentional mindfulness skills that Ed could use in real time; as both mindfulness and therapeutic art brought considerable insights, this was also to help develop creative strategies to process deeper emotions through his interest in photography. These strategies were aligned to Ed's personal and creative sensibilities for working things out.

Beginning with an ACT values worksheet that highlighted life domains in relation to fulfillment and need (Harris, 2008), Ed was able to gain a clearer picture of how his work and life were out of balance. Seeing this on paper also led him to notice that he "wasn't being true to himself." he disliked his current job that required a "cut-throat" approach, and he also missed working with his former team, many of whom he was still friends with. Borrowing from Russ Harris's hexaflex format (Harris, 2009), we mindfully processed and diffused Ed's rage and grief which were most pronounced at the time. As a homework exercise, I suggested that Ed might want to choose a poignant photograph and write about what it meant to him, and what stood out most.

Ed arrived at the next session with three photos, having responded to the brief. The first photograph was just after his redundancy and he recalled how difficult it was to go on holiday. Most of the photographs didn't have people in them, but the first one he showed me was of a bicycle leaning against a doorway. This reminded Ed that even during that difficult time, he still had support from his wife as well as the grounding of a nurturing childhood when his father, all those years ago, empathically reminded Ed to calm himself with a breath. Along similar lines, the second photograph was of go-karting with his daughter, reminding Ed of the many enjoyable moments in life that he can anchor to when feeling overwhelmed.

Figure 12.1 The old burnt-out car (see color plate)

The third photograph (Figure 12.1), which stood out most to him and was more whimsical, was an old burnt-out car, symbolizing to Ed "the transition from something functional that suddenly becomes an art form. It stood the test of time…and still serves a purpose." For the first time, Ed was able to see a degree of humor with regard to himself, the car, and his situation. Not to minimize the impact of it, but to lighten the mood, and find a moment of relief from worrying.

Although Ed had not necessarily thought about these things at the time of taking the photographs, he was now able to see them in a new light. Being open meant he no longer needed to fear his emotions, or avoid them. And reflecting on the images with greater flexibility enabled Ed to reclaim his self-worth, and a sense of the things he valued most in life.

Summing up

Ed was already seasoned in using the breath to calm himself down when he first came to therapy, but less so in knowing how to deal with deep-felt emotions that bubbled under the surface. His goal for therapy was to learn how to regulate his emotions over four sessions. The combination of ACT mindfulness and creative scripting through photographic images provided him with a set of tools to do so.

The ACT skills provided Ed with a set of strategies for confronting rather than burying his feelings, or getting caught up by negative moods. He was able to allow for them when anchored to what he valued most in life, a supportive family. By diffusing threatening emotions, they seemed to lose their power. Similarly, Ed could use his penchant for photography to process low or anxious moods through images. Doing so enabled him to explore his angst with sensitivity and playfulness and begin to see the "extraordinary in the ordinary" (Peterson, 1998).

This combined skill set was in accord with Ed's personal sensitivities and sensibilities. He was one of those clients who came with firm goals and sought only four sessions. In line with this demeanor, he worked resourcefully in and outside of each one. While not all clients work that fast, I have found that using strategies that feel most natural to clients is an important part of the therapeutic process.

CHAPTER 13

Complementary Methods

Art therapy and mindfulness methods as healing agents were considered to be an adjunct to therapy only a decade or so ago (Walsh and Shapiro, 2006). Nowadays, they are recognized as valid forms of complementary therapy that contribute to mind–body health (NIMH, 2014). An ongoing interest in the healing effects of consciousness has contributed to this shift, as research and practice in metapsychology, guided imagery, mindfulness and art therapy have gradually progressed. Although these methods are sometimes difficult to prove empirically, their health-enhancing effects are widely reported. In addition, health consumers are increasingly coming to value their benefits as genuine or meaningful (NMH, 2014).

Metapsychology

Peter Levine (2010) in *An Unspoken Voice* suggests that the power and role of consciousness are typically underestimated in healing, particularly in terms of understanding the role of unconscious processes that shut down when people feel threatened or scared. In asserting that people have the capacity to heal trauma and associated fears within them, Levine argues that we can learn to circumvent biological or emotional shutdown when we integrate sensory and emotional experience into a coherent whole. Similar to the basic tenets of mindfulness, the notion of noticing "what I am experiencing now" can result in the discovery of the inner world through emotional memories and sensory experiences that dominate our thoughts, feelings, perceptions, beliefs, and actions.

Understanding feelings is at the heart of therapy. The felt sense communicates important somatic markers in relation to our emotional literacy, and how emotional memories play out in our lives (Levine, 2010). Laury Rappaport (2009), in combining Eugene Gendlin's notion of the felt sense (a shift in physical sensation linked to thoughts or emotions) with creative empowerment, has developed a mind–body approach to art therapy that invites one to an awareness of inner experience "in the now." By adopting a focusing attitude (compassion, openness, acceptance), Rappaport has developed a method for witnessing and welcoming deep-felt emotional experience and expressing it through art. As an approach to wholeness, "noticing" is central to the method as it guides clients to connect with bodily shifts linked to emotions and express them through symbolic "handles" (word, phrase, gesture, sound). These help people acknowledge and detach from core issues that keep them stuck, and they can begin to move forward through integrated experiential learning (Rappaport, 2009).

The late transpersonal psychologist Dr. Jeanne Achterberg (1942–2012), an early pioneer in the field of mind–body medicine, similarly sought to capture the invisible forces of consciousness and healing through things like prayer and visualization. Based on an accumulating body of evidence to show that subtle, invisible realms, though difficult to pinpoint, contribute to healing. Achterberg guided cancer patients through contemplative and spiritual practices (such as prayer, imagery and ritual) to facilitate healing (1994, 2008). By focusing attention on intentions to heal, Achterberg found that integrated consciousness through imagery positively affected health and well-being. Though not all patients recovered, some did, and many were able to move from states of fear or resignation to making peace with their illness (Achterberg, 2008).

The combination of traditional and modern methods of healing through guided imagery has found its way into contemporary therapeutic art settings. This emanates largely from notions about the restorative powers of art (Henderson and Gladding, 1998), restorative tacit rituals (Levine, 2005), and an understanding about the spiritual aspects of shamanic healing (McNiff, 2004). Although these methods differ cross-culturally, the common thread is that many people believe in the phenomena (Rubin, 2005).

These approaches serve to galvanize methods for accessing inner wisdom and they attempt to help people heal through deeper powers of consciousness. The language of art can be difficult to capture empirically, but not in felt emotion. Emotions are the universal language of art. In a therapeutic sense, art moves people beyond ordinary consciousness and into the heart of the matter where emotions give voice to deeper awareness and intentions.

Decentering through mindful art

Meditative mindfulness in the silent phase of therapy can bolster inner knowing through the power of "decentering." Decentering (mental distancing) occurs naturally when we daydream, get caught up in the mood of our favorite music, or walk out of a room and suddenly remember where we put our car keys. When we mentally distance ourselves from the normal way we think about things, we can engage deeper levels of consciousness that connect us to truth, nature, and spirit through free play or art.

Beyond the relaxation of calming meditation, the process is restorative in that we can, even if only momentarily, "let go" of our defenses. When we stop striving, we can naturally step back from trying to control things. We gain perspective. In these moments, we can free up rigid styles of thinking and approach problems with creative power. Drawing on our intuition, inner knowing and our natural sensibilities enables us to "get lost in the game" through art and self-discovery (Winnicott, 1971). As such, we can become more sensitive and compassionate to our life experience through the aesthetic propensity of mindful art therapy.

Nikisha

Following a meditative art task, Nikisha reflected on her image of two trees with a wavy, diving line down the center to represent the contrast between feelings of empowerment and loss of control. As can sometimes happen, our session had been interrupted during the guided meditation, and we had a limited amount of time in which to finish.

Reflecting on the image, Nikisha paraphrased Goethe, remarking how "sometimes our life resembles a cool tree in winter who would notice those leaves would turn again…but we hope we will know it. [In relation to the interruption] like we can't control time…but we can control what we do with our time." Streamlining the aesthetic dimensions of both the artwork (line, shape, form, color) and our therapy in the moment (being interrupted, thrown off course), we remained image-centered in exploring the inner tensions of Nikisha's artwork that mirrored the issues she was grappling with at the time.

Summing up

In this chapter, the emphasis has been on how mindfulness combines with creative activity to decenter through art. The capacity to mentally distance oneself from ordinary logic bolsters creative energy, and the capacity to go with the flow. Decentering through the aesthetic dimensions (therapeutic and psychological) contributed further to the power of creativity. For Nikisha, both mindfulness and art were significant and gainful.

Furthermore, the dividing line between the trees seemed to end her struggle in some way. Whereas mental distancing through meditative mindfulness facilitated mental clarity, the interruption of the session may have contributed as a therapeutic mirror in which to balance inner tensions (Betensky, 1995). On the whole, Nikisha worked within her inner sensibilities where paying attention with intention was creative, achievable, and in the moment. Mindful reflection and direct experiencing took place in all phases of the task, including during contemplation, art-making, and mindful reflection. Without resorting to a preconceived theory for interpretation, we were able to see the woods for the trees.

CHAPTER 14

Mindful-Based Stress Reduction (MBSR) for Wellness

It goes without saying that reflecting on past experience can arouse emotional memories. But if a past experience was difficult or challenging in some way, just thinking about it can cause the brain to respond automatically with the same feelings of anxiety and physical health symptoms (Kabat-Zinn, 1990; Oyan, 2003). However, being present and aware can lessen arousal so that feeling and being nervous have less power. As the next case study shows, turning inward through mindfulness and expressing through art enabled this client to detach from emotional refuse and begin to visualize his health and well-being.

Luke

Luke, a 26-year-old man, was referred by his GP for generalized anxiety (GAD) and irritable bowel syndrome (IBS). He had previously attended therapy employing desensitization methods, which he found ineffective, and he hoped art therapy might help.

Luke had been experiencing severe stomach cramps for the past year or so that prevented him from engaging in social activities and often resulted in a day or two off work each week. He explained that the IBS symptoms were immobilizing and associated with stress, but they were reduced or ameliorated once the stress triggers were removed (i.e., anticipating an exam brings them on, after the exam, they dissipate). Cognizant of both his emotional triggers and capacity for recovery (though conditional), Luke felt as though he were on a roller coaster between the inner tensions of worry and the outer demands of needing to perform where he functioned through his "drive and willpower."

Exploring freedom

Following a guided meditation, Luke's first image was of a cross within a circle, which he said represented the difficulty he experienced in saying "no" to people. Aware of his acquiescent nature, Luke didn't want to let anyone down. However, he found himself giving too much and, despite understanding the need to be more assertive, he struggled with this. Both metaphorically and literally, he took to the image again, transforming it this time into "how he would like things to be." Reflecting on the revisions, Luke reasoned that he had choices, that he "no longer had a cross to bear...it's now a butterfly...more freeing from this perspective. It was unintentional, but seemed to be what worked...freedom."

In the next session, Luke's image characterized the inner divisions he felt between the debilitating effects of IBS symptoms and his need to function. Connecting with the felt sense of his condition, Luke explained that the IBS symptoms "start with tightness ... heartburn and my stomach locks and the feeling is tight and burning. Once stress is over the symptoms are removed with it." But then he explained how he managed to function through his "willfulness and drive." Luke drew an ocean scene where he used color resourcefully to delineate between sensory feelings. He explained that

> the worst feeling is red [anxiety and tension]...the tight, tense spasms of the stomach...I imagined washing it away. Blue water was stronger going back out to sea...gentler [lighter blue] coming in. Toward the end I saw yellow...a shifting...like in hypnosis...like...[representing] freedom from resistance, when the mind won't let go.

As the sessions progressed, Luke began to cultivate a daily meditation practice at home as well as in therapy. Throughout this time he used art to symbolically express and chart his progress. Stress was debilitating and the IBS symptoms continued to immobilize him, keeping him from work and taking part in the sport activities that he enjoyed (particularly competition tennis with friends on the weekend). However, over the next few weeks, Luke's symptoms slowly began to improve. He was also becoming more mindful of how "worry" robbed him of his vitality and capacity to engage with others.

Figure 14.1 Feeling trapped/cage (see color plate)

The cage with an open door represented feelings of being trapped in a job he didn't like, but also didn't know how to leave at the time. Luke said it's "of a prison cage with black bars...but the door is open now because there is a choice [of another job]." He feared risking the repercussions of giving notice to a difficult boss, as well as beginning a new job that represented uncertainty. As Luke explained, "the prison is extended to life in general...in terms of everything. It would be better if...I don't take the opportunity for change...then I would know everything...like what to do...where to be...and I would know what to expect." The fear of giving notice was also compounded by the fear of "burning his bridges" and the uncertainty should the new job not work out. Nonetheless, Luke inherently *knew* that the shift from one job to the other was the right move. He was just uncomfortable with change.

In a spontaneous image, an absence of cages represented the idea that Luke had again had a shift in his thinking. In this image, elements of nature and color combined to give rise to green grass (relaxing) and yellow sunshine (hope) amidst blue (ocean waves). These Luke said were to "restore vitality, heal immunity, and gain freedom from stress." To Luke, this represented the possibility of a brighter future if he could learn to take control of his anxiety. He was attempting to do this through breath and positive intentions.

Several sessions later, Luke produced a trio of images that seemed to move beyond critical thinking and penetrate deeper levels of consciousness. In all three, kinesthetic lines visually and conceptually expressed his deeper concerns across a trajectory of feelings that were embodied within a tight knot in his gut. These symptoms represented an impenetrable state of fear shielded by perfectionism that guarded his self-worth. The first was a sketch of a man with a large parcel on his back, much like a heavy knapsack that seemed to be weighing him down. This image represented a general sense of Luke "feeling like there is something on my back."

In the second image, Luke produced a single word written in the middle of the page, which was underlined: "dread." Luke began by explaining the sensory quality of it, before moving on to the visual image that articulated it. Luke said:

> It's like there is a mental block and I can't think properly... then I get an upset stomach and generalized anxiety where my heart speeds up, and I have a slight tremor in my hands...and then I feel a headache coming on.

Then he explained the dread of going to work, being at work, and the need for perfectionism. As we explored this theme further, Luke explained a long history of perfectionism, and that he had experienced IBS symptoms since his final university exams. Although this was already a few years ago, and that Luke was currently working in a supportive environment with opportunities to specialize and achieve in his field, he remained anxious and unsure whenever he thought about his work.

This single word "dread" was accompanied by another image shaped squarely and filled with scribbles that seemed to represent a jumble of wire. A cross (also scribbled) diagonally wended its way beneath and atop the shape. Luke described this image in relation to his recent bout of flu representing "the black hole...and feeling sick this past week; it was all encompassing...everything a void." We stayed with this image, further exploring the history and trajectory of dread across the next session. Subsequently, Luke shaded green over two-thirds of the image to illustrate that there were times when he felt relaxed, for example while at home or walking the dog near the river. The green highlighting nature represented the nearby parks which he frequented and where he found solace. A prominent red dot in the center of the image referred to Luke's "worries about the future; his capacity to perform well at work, and to survive general health."

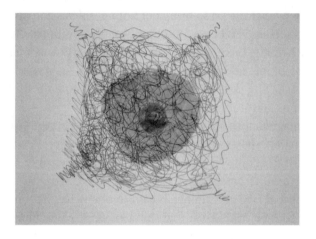

Figure 14.2 Dread (see color plate)

Summing up

Occupational stress is commonplace these days. Notwithstanding the possibility of a toxic working environment, debilitating work stress, if left unchecked can contribute to more enduring forms of anxiety. Although Luke left a "toxic" workplace a few weeks after our first session, he remained traumatized for several months afterwards. During the transition to his new job, he felt emotionally stuck and found it difficult to trust that things would be better, even though he liked the work, and his new boss seemed welcoming and supportive. Furthermore, Luke was still in contact with his former co-workers, and although he didn't feel responsible for their welfare, he felt somewhat guilty when they filled his ear with their ongoing complaints and disgruntlement with the old workplace.

As Luke began to connect with the emotional and physical sense of "feeling stuck," the therapeutic process enabled him to entertain the idea of emotional freedom and physical relief. Consistent with the idea that change and healing from trauma require a person to deal with "body sensations, emotions and the totality of experience" (Levine, 2010), Luke used the breath to calm himself, guided meditation to explore felt emotions and body sensations, and the creative power of the art to bring out both problems and possibilities for change. The silent power of the art brought additional therapeutic gains in helping Luke to move beyond ordinary reasoning to felt awareness of his IBS symptoms. The butterfly, in response to his notion of having a cross to bear, seemed to conjure up hope of freedom and transformation.

The imaginal shift from feeling trapped in a prison cage to a calming scene of nature shows the beginnings of psychological flexibility and a desire for freedom. This took place when Luke began to reappraise worry (shifting from *what if...*) to an open attitude (*so what if...*) that he paired with a calming breath. Nonetheless, it took several weeks before he could trust that the new work environment would remain positive "beyond the honeymoon period." In Luke's mind, he was still working to release "three years of learned behavior and maladaptive coping," which he found difficult to let go of.

However, Luke's image of dread seemed to mark a turning point for him, owing to insights about his deeper lack of self-worth. Beyond conceptual reasoning where he feared his work might not be good enough, Luke learned to sense the mounting tension of IBS symptoms, which he could at least partially manage with breath and intention. Reducing symptoms was one of his goals for therapy. Gradually requiring less medication, Luke found that daily practice of meditation was helping to prevent and relieve his symptoms. Added to this, we began working on his emotional compass to guide self-acceptance where Luke gradually acknowledged that he was learning to "become his own best friend."

CHAPTER 15

Acceptance and Commitment Therapy (ACT)

Acceptance and Commitment Therapy (ACT) arose from the Dialectical Behavior Therapy (DBT) and the work of Marsha Linehan and colleagues (1993/2014). They combined cognitive behavioral and Buddhist mindfulness methods (acceptance, present-moment awareness) to treat clients suffering from borderline personality disorder. Clients are taught the psychosocial aspects of living, and how to regulate emotions in the physical and relational environment through exposure to and mindful awareness of automatic and dysfunctional thoughts. This helps people learn to become aware of the energy and actions they bring to their activities. Learning to focus on the present moment rather than splitting one's attention between past or future is integral to recovery and transforming the inner dialogue adaptively (Linehan, 1993/2014).

ACT emanated in part from this work in conjunction with relational frame theory (contextual therapy) (Fletcher, Shoendorff and Hayes, 2010). Popularized by Steven Hayes and colleagues as an experiential approach to cognitive behavioral therapy, the theory expands on conventional therapy by way of the general idea of a user-friendly approach to teaching people to take action or "act" when feeling stuck. Utilizing the core mindfulness qualities of openness and acceptance, ACT has been integrated into mainstream therapy for both high- and low-functioning clients as a means of fostering psychological flexibility in light of life's inevitable challenges.

Although the core processes are interrelated, the foundational strategy for ACT is acceptance. By accepting painful experience and reframing it within a context of personal values, clients can move closer, with presence and detachment, toward the things that cause pain. Through a series of brief attentional strategies, people are taught to diffuse from physical or emotional pain, accept them as part of life, and reorient to the self-in-context within the present moment (Kashdin and Harris, 2013). Allowing painful experience to exist side-by-side with positive experience contributes to psychological flexibility and helps people detach from painful experience, and refocus their energy toward meaningful life choices (Harris, 2008).

As with *MBSR* programs, ACT mindfulness is central to intervention through interrelated processes of present-moment awareness, acceptance, detachment, non-judgment, and the observing self. While meditative practice is not part of the protocol, the ACT concept of values echoes the eightfold Buddhist path of wisdom which consists of "right mindfulness, right concentration, right view, right intention, right speech, right action, right living and right effort" (Kramer, 2007 in Fletcher *et al.*, 2010, p.43). These are reflected in specific, core ACT practices that attempt to shape thinking and language used in everyday experience (Kashdin and Ciarrochi, 2013).

Being open and accepting instead of trying to change another person or situation can be freeing. When we stop struggling, problems have less power, and our capacity to tolerate negative experience increases (Harris, 2008). This involves a conscious decision to actively and receptively allow both positive and negative life experiences to be part of our lives (Hayes *et al.*, 1999). However, acceptance does not necessarily mean liking or approving of what we think and feel, nor does it mean tolerating unfair or abusive situations. It's simply about witnessing painful or difficult experience without getting caught up in it (Eifert, Forsyth and McKay, 2006). As difficult as it can be to let go of painful emotions, or stop trying to reconcile an injustice, clients can learn to stop struggling with things like strong emotions or physical symptoms, and begin to regulate their responses by learning to become present and aware.

Perspective-taking via an ACT hexaflex is central to guiding clients through six core processes of the method in order to achieve psychological flexibility (acceptance, cognitive fusion, being present, self as context, values, committed action). In several instances, I have found that dialoguing around the hexaflex (Harris) seems to help clients anchor their thoughts in valued and meaningful directions. This not only enables people to accept the balance of positive and negative life experience, but working with values also enables them to flourish in ways that are personally significant. Other resources that help to anchor meaningful action are the values worksheet that highlights major life domains (love, work, health, leisure). This helps clients to reappraise areas of need and fulfillment (Harris, 2008).

Imaginative metaphors are often incorporated in ACT intervention to help people anchor to and map out present-moment experience in a detached way. Like stories, metaphors can lead to insights about the real problem because they capture a network of associated memories, feelings, images, and events that symbolize a person's values, identity, and relationship patterns (Rennie, 2002). In art, these are sometimes worked through privately (Rubin, 2005). Moreover, metaphors can act in concert with images because they help capture the essence of emotion-based associations, and forge links between subjective and objective experience. The following case study illustrates how this client made use of ACT intervention. This guided her to "act" on what matters most, and consequently began to transform her depleted energy levels.

Claire

Claire, a 30-year-old woman, was referred by her GP for depleted energy levels. She had been feeling generally "weak, fuzzy, dizzy and hot," and was frustrated by her overall lack of energy. Although chronic fatigue was ruled out, Claire also suffered from sleep apnea so a lack of restorative sleep may have contributed to chronic fatigue and poor concentration, weight gain, and back pain. Depression (21=severe), anxiety (3=normal), and stress (18=mild) were scored on intake in accordance with the Depression, Anxiety and Stress Scale (DASS) (Lovibond and Lovibond, 1995). Claire was most frustrated with her inability to keep up with normal daily activities. At the time, she had just relocated back to town and was caring for her three-year-old toddler, while also attempting to complete her studies.

Although taking time out for a mid-day nap seemed near impossible, Claire was nonetheless proactive in attempting to manage her health issues and raise her energy levels. Coming to therapy was part of this plan, as was attending clinical Pilates and regular visits to her GP and chiropractor. Reasoning that conventional psychotherapy had already provided her with opportunities to "talk over everything that needed to be said," Claire was interested in combining mindfulness and art-therapy skills to manage her low energy levels.

In the early stages of therapy, Claire practiced mindful breathing to calm her frustration and engage with mind–body presence. At home, she paired breath work with brief periods of relaxation, while resting her back against an orthopedic cushion. Although respite was often limited to a few minutes at a time, Claire did this several times a day in order to stop and regroup before proceeding with the next activity. It was a matter of quality time, rather than quantity. In therapy, we used guided meditations, followed by an art task to provide Claire with opportunities to explore the deeper essence of her exhaustion. Her early works, sketched simply in colored magic markers, were often accompanied by words to emphasize the meaning. The underlying theme of these images over the next few months represented a lifetime of feeling undervalued and misunderstood.

In one of her earlier images (not shown here), thick bright orange lines surrounding the neck and voice box of a lone purple figure stood in the middle of the page. Although the figure lacked facial features, this was more representative of Claire's personal style of drawing through simple shapes and colors highlighted by key words, rather than a lack of identity or direction. Below the figure, the words "frustration, misunderstood, undervalued," also in bright orange, attested to the anguish that drained Claire's energy and left her feeling overwhelmed. The contrast of color and form between the purple figure (a favored color), and bright orange (a less preferred color), provided an aesthetic clue to the whole of Claire's experience where her lack of being heard and validated overwhelmed, and left her feeling obstructed.

In another image (not shown here) entitled *Exhaustion*, Claire produced two concentric circles containing the words "exhaustion, crash, overwhelmed" to describe what she was feeling internally at the time. The words "stress, pain, overloaded, avoidance, and nurturing" were written along the outer circle and described her outer reality, owing to current life demands and a depletion of energy. Nurturing represented both her obligation to nurture others and a need for self-nurturing which resulted in withdrawing from life whenever she could. Reflecting on this image, Claire realized that despite her desire and attempts to bolster her resilience, when things threatened to overwhelm her, she typically needed to withdraw her energy.

Several sessions later, Claire's energy began to pick up. She seemed visibly more alert and relaxed, and mentioned that she was keen to integrate ACT skills into art therapy. Following a brief guided meditation, Claire produced a visual storyboard of both the problem and solution regarding her feelings of exhaustion.

Figure 15.1 Storyboard of exhaustion and a means out of it

Claire's storyboard of exhaustion and a means out of it

Across the six panes, beginning at the left upper hand corner, Claire described the sensation of being exhausted as "like being on a boat, caught in a storm." This, she said, was the larger sense of feeling overwhelmed. As she said, "I feel sick in the storm and there's little motivation. The problem here is recovery." Moving across the page, the next two frames at the top represent a sense of "floating, just drifting, without direction, motivation, energy or drive." The one in the middle is a detail of the one on the right that embodies feeling lost. As Claire explained, "I don't know where I am, I don't have energy or direction."

The stars on the bottom left represent the "drive to find your way. The stars tell you how to get back to shore" through what you value most in life. The images in the bottom middle and right depicted by boats with oars, where the middle is a detail of the one on the right, use breath and intention to return to valued living. Claire explained that the "oars represent the breath, and breath helps you row back to shore."

Summing up her artwork, Claire saw the image as a holistic perspective of the power of mindfulness, through breath, stillness, and creative solutions that could help her bolster inner resources, and assist in her recovery from chronic exhaustion. As we explored this artwork further by dialoguing with an ACT approach, we reviewed Claire's intentions for valued living across the life domains of health, relationships, work, and leisure. This enabled Claire to reflect consciously on the negative thoughts and behaviors that drained her energy, as well as on her positive strengths and inner resourcefulness. On the whole, Claire was able to gauge her energy levels across each domain, and consider how best to transform her exhaustion. In doing so, Claire used mindful art therapy as a foundation for exploring the areas of life where she felt stuck, and keep herself on track.

Summing up

Beyond conventional talk therapy, Claire found a prescription for living through mindful art therapy. Breath work became a versatile and potent tool for soothing her frustration, and help her get back on track when feeling overwhelmed. Decentering through contemplative mindfulness and creative activities provided her with further tools with which to be present with her feelings (exhaustion) and explore the deeper aspects of it. Rather than resist her frustration, Claire came to accept her emotional and sensory experience, but not to identify with it.

For Claire, mindfulness and art were significant and gainful. Where trying to make logical sense of chronic exhaustion seemed futile, decentering mindfully and collaboratively through art provided opportunities to explore new discoveries about the sense and meaning of it. Moreover, aesthetic reflections beyond the obvious content of the image enabled Claire to comprehend more deeply how she used her energy. Much like a solid tree (another of her images representing inner strength), Claire found the method helped to ground her in her sensibilities and provide her with fresh insights. When Claire felt it was time to terminate therapy, we paired an ACT mindfulness protocol with a favorite art and craft activity so that if ever Claire wanted to explore sensory or emotional experience outside of the sessions' creativity, she could do so.

CHAPTER 16

Positive Psychology

At a recent community lecture on positive psychology, the speaker introduced a familiar catch phrase: "control > alt > delete." He went on to explain that this represented the sentiments of an acquaintance who framed her disability as follows: "I can control my thoughts > there are always alternatives to how I see things > and I can choose to delete what I don't need." This was her attempt to utilize positive strengths and develop a foundation for wellness in light of her recent adjustment to a disability.

Positive psychology, introduced by Seligman and Csikszentmihalyi (2000), is a corrective response to psychology's emphasis on pathology. The main aim is to develop a focus on wellness—rather than disorder—in order to capture a more realistic appraisal of life experience and what it means to be human. At the subjective level, the field of positive psychology focuses on valued experiences, well-being, life satisfaction, and hope. From a personal view, this entails a focus on positive individual traits, and from a group level, valued citizenship (Kashdin and Ciarrochi, 2013).

Positive psychology is often referred to as the "science of happiness." But happiness doesn't mean that everything in life will necessarily be good, happy, or desirable. In the normal scheme of things, we have a balance of positive and negative life experience. Furthermore, our innate bias toward survival means that we tend to gravitate toward and focus on negative experience when they happen (Hanson, 2013).

In positive psychology, mindfulness helps to increase equanimity and concentration by focusing on character strengths to mobilize resources, and cultivate health and well-being. Whereas earlier proponents of positive psychology focused mainly on positive and negative strengths, and attributes to effect change, more recent followers have sought a more dynamic approach to well-being. Moving beyond superficial notions of positive and negative experience, practitioners now tend to adopt the approach of focusing on all elements that may lead a person to living well. For example, people who suffer from anxiety often use control strategies (rituals, routines) to ensure they will not have to face what they fear or feel uncomfortable with. These avoidance strategies, if successful, soon become habitual and automatic, reinforcing maladaptive cycles of negative or catastrophic self-talk. This is where mindfulness can be used skillfully to show clients how they can replace their need for control (avoidance) with the capacity to take control (adaptive coping).

A useful metaphor in this instance might be to suggest that a client see themselves as the director of a play taking place in the mind. They can choose which thoughts play center stage, which are just out of sight in the wings, or which get banished to the backstage! Noticing thoughts, feelings, and sensations is the first step in becoming present and developing a relationship with the internal world. Making choices about how to respond is the second, and affects how we relate in the world. Though seemingly paradoxical, by drawing on a client's need for control (rigid thinking), their proficiency for control can also be used as a strength or sensibility for skillfully enhancing cognitive flexibility.

Veronica

Veronica, a woman in her fifties, came to therapy to sort out "what she wanted in life." This was her goal. Having recently retired as a carer for elderly end-of-life patients, she was emotionally burnt out. Veronica was keen to explore and develop her "authentic self" in therapy. On the one hand, Veronica sensed that "she was blocked by her ego;" on the other, she felt that "she didn't know what she wanted to do, or how to change her life." Her frustration was palpable when she spoke of it.

In the first session, Veronica struggled to calm her anxiety, but eventually did so by attempting to engage in breath work. When the guided meditation finished, her pent-up frustration spilled onto the page in swirling red and black chaos that resembled the shape and character of a tornado (Figure 16.1).

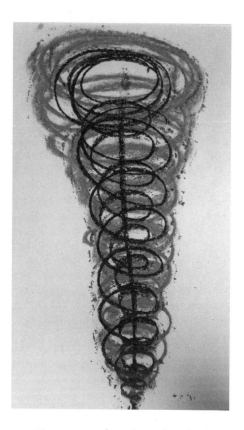

Figure 16.1 Chaos (see color plate)

Bold, sweeping circles embodied the frustration of key childhood events whose resonance continued to play out in her life. Reflecting on the image, Veronica seemed in a rush to disclose past events so she could move on from them. She mentioned that she was ready to shed the outdated feelings embodied in this artwork in favor of transforming it in ways that "would make life better." She then asked if she could continue to work on the image.

Despite the importance of processing this first image with Veronica, I equally sensed the urgency with which she seemed to need to move forward with it. Fortunately, with the advent of photography, I was able to capture the first image shown here (embodied frustration) before Veronica spontaneously transformed it into "something more positive and hopeful" in a matter of minutes.

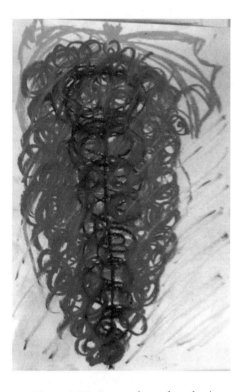

Figure 16.2 Grapes (see color plate)

This second image (Figure 16.2) represents "the fruit of life [grapes], complete with light [sunshine] and personal growth [leaves]." Reflecting on the image gave Veronica hope and confidence that the possibilities for change were within her. Consistent with current trends in neuroscience and positive psychology, this shows how clients can begin to attempt to hold positive and negative emotions simultaneously in order to develop adaptive emotional responding (Hanson, 2009; 2013).

Both images provided crucial symbols for exploring the inner division between Veronica's frustration and hope. Highlighting both the problem and the solution, we explored the dichotomies of how life threatened to spiral out of control contrasted with Veronica's innate sense of hope that it wouldn't and her capacity for resilience.

Summing up

Through concerted efforts to calm herself mindfully, Veronica was able to access the deeper energy of her frustration and begin to reflect without attaching to it. Processing the psychological and therapeutic aesthetic dimensions through art was important in providing a context for exploring the energy she brought to it. Her ongoing visual dialogue through spontaneity—from the first image to the second—further provided Veronica with opportunities for authentic disclosure through the power of the images. By tangibly expressing past and future, this helped bridge the ambiguity between thinking, feeling, and behavior and also illustrates how art provides a visual voice when thoughts rush in or ideas overwhelm.

Landgarten's (1975) notion of personal symbology comes to mind here in highlighting the importance of clients sharing their personal meanings in therapy. But this begs the question: "Are strengths inherently positive?" (Kashdin and Ciarrochi, 2013, p.39). Aesthetic dimensions of therapy enabled Veronica to be free through the art, whereas both images highlighted the emotional tensions that competed for "living authentically," which was Veronica's goal for therapy.

The contrast between image one (frustration) and image two (resilience) gave us a tangible basis through which to instill some mindfulness principles of positive psychology to foster her resilience despite past and present disappointments. An awareness of the positive life experiences and attributes in which to anchor this resilience enabled Veronica to begin to free herself from the negative energy that threatened to overwhelm, and keep her stuck in the past.

Transforming the original image into something more valued (signaling her need to get it right and move on) (McNiff, 2004), enabled Veronica to reflect simultaneously on old issues, new strivings, and create a direction for moving forward. This path for authentic disclosure enabled Veronica to capture a network of memories, associations, events, and feelings through the images (Rennie, 2002). This marked a point where our "true" therapy could begin.

PART FIVE

Developing a Mindful Art-Therapy Practice

CHAPTER 17

On Becoming a Mindful Art Therapist

Relational empathy

In *On Becoming a Person*, Carl Rogers (1995) notes that "the degree to which I can create relationships, which facilitate the growth of others as separate persons, is a measure of the growth I have achieved in myself" (p.56). Most therapists will be familiar with Roger's person-centered therapy (1980) which espouses the core skills of empathy (understanding the world from the client's view), unconditional positive regard (acceptance), and genuineness (authenticity and sharing feelings). More than just skills, these comprise an interpersonal process for the therapeutic relationship, whereby clients who feel heard and validated, without fear of reprisal, also feel accepted and valued by the therapist. Feeling valued fosters self-empathy and brings self-compassion to bear on one's experience and capacity for problem-solving. Clients consequently grow through the process.

Rogers (1960), in *A Way of Being*, also suggests that this non-directive style of therapy is more about learning to "be with" a client, rather than needing to "do therapy." Relational empathy shares in the mindful attitude of being present and witnessing another human's suffering with openness and acceptance. This results in psychological safety. In the absence of needing to defend experience, clients often gain a greater sense of their own humanness, and begin to develop self-compassion. The calming effects of feeling accepted not only serve to slow mind chatter, but also offers psychological safety. Regardless of whether a client's problem stems from difficult relationships or life events, the forgiveness of self and of others is an area that people struggle with if they stay caught up in the story. In the presence of a mindful therapist, clients can stop beating themselves or others up, or stop focusing on things like blame or victimization. Instead, they can turn gently or courageously toward the deeper meaning of life's challenges without feeling judged. But, you might be wondering at this stage, what's art got to do with it?

The empathic resonance between therapist and client borrows from humanist perspectives that affirm one's capacity to progress adaptively in life through valued living. Relational empathy enables a therapist to remain objective and image-centered, rather than self-centered in the therapeutic dialogue (Buie, 1981). Empathic awareness also helps therapists untangle the emotional charge of a client's artwork (Franklin, 1990). In the broader realm, where value is placed on the client and his or her world, relational empathy serves both the way we engage with clients, as well as with their art.

Developing a mindful art-therapy practice

Developing a mindful art-therapy practice is less about the choice of mindfulness techniques or creative art forms you introduce, and more about cultivating a practice that resonates personally and professionally. There is no "one size fits all" (NIMH, 2014), nor will one style of therapy suit all clients. Although it is wise to have a loose plan, a theoretical basis, or starting point for therapy, one never knows what a client's needs will be on the very day.

If you are keen to introduce mindful art therapy into your practice, it is wise to cultivate mindfulness skills and art-based endeavors. Secular mindfulness methods can vary according to the practitioner, therapeutic approach, or the sensibilities of a client. Depending on how well versed you are already, this might require you to familiarize yourself with meditative and cognitive attentional mindfulness practices which you can then combine with creative art tasks.

When I introduced mindfulness skills to a couple recently, one partner remarked of the other: "She's too much like a hummingbird." Understanding clients in terms of their nature and readiness to engage with sensitive material is important if you want to introduce skillful therapy. As Malchiodi (2003/5) notes, therapists need to discern how methods might facilitate or distance a person in accordance with their readiness. If clients are hesitant about the method, it is important to explore why or whether mindful art therapy is a good fit.

One of the most important aspects of therapy I have found is to engage the sensibilities of my clients. Some may enjoy the quietude of meditation, while others may prefer using only cognitive attentional strategies to dialogue with the art.

Being attuned to a person's creative interests or abilities can also help to tailor the focus of guided meditations or art tasks. For example, when Sophia asked if she could read a poem entitled *The Door* (Holub, 2007), I was able to follow up with a guided meditation to assist her imaginatively in finding the courage to move through the door, and explore the unfinished business she had come to discuss. This is not to suggest that all guided meditations need be tailored to the individual, for whether you are listening to a John Kabat-Zinn meditation or develop one spontaneously, the idea is to guide clients to a space of relaxed and open awareness, within imaginative metaphors, where they can witness and explore inner mental life through it.

Clients come from a range of backgrounds and interests, so I typically ask about their hobbies and interests on the client intake form. This information can guide creative activities in ways that make sense to your client, and that they can relate to more easily. In addition to drawing tasks, I have found it useful to engage clients mindfully with compelling photographs, collage, drama or poetry that they find meaningful. When creative tasks resonate personally with clients, they are often keen to explore emotions through them. For example, when we drew on Ed's love of photography to explore the "extraordinary in the ordinary" of compelling images, it brought him closer in emotionally. Familiar and favored techniques that engage a client's sensibilities not only enhance therapeutic gains, but are also easily transferrable for use outside of therapy.

Often, if clients feel stuck or don't know what to draw, I suggest they may like to sketch the same image three times, and color each one differently (Fausek, 1997). More often than not, the first image will be realistic, the second a bit more uncharacteristic from the norm, and the third tends to show the beginnings of becoming more experimental. Even without an obvious motive to resolve anything, this activity marks a shift in emotional involvement with the original task, and encourages psychological flexibility. For example, in exploring new ways of looking at something or learning to tolerate ambiguity (Rogers, 1961).

CHAPTER 18

A Note About Music

It goes without saying that music is powerful—you can take a trip through the 1970s, compose a meal to the tune of Bach, or kick back to the sounds of nature. Music is a personal thing and often a powerful means for disengaging from stress. Over the last several years, I have introduced background music to therapy to enhance relaxation and deepen the inward turn. Most of the music has been selected from a range of ambient tunes or neuroacoustic brain entrainment music to enhance alpha and theta relaxation. This style of music seems to me to overlap with mindfulness methods that attempt to enhance relaxation through adaptive neuroplasticity.

Along the same lines, the background music for the guided meditation *Ocean Breath*, which is included with this book, was produced with the aim of enhancing alpha-theta relaxation. Two tracks are included: one with guided meditation, and one with music only. MP3 files of this guided meditation and music can be found at the following link: www.jkp.com/mindful-art-therapy.html.

Ocean breath: Guided meditation script[1]

This is a time for relaxation…a time to go within…
Relax your mind and body, and let go of anything that's
worrying you…
Begin now…by focusing on your breathing…

---

1 Disclaimer: this guided meditation is intended for relaxation. Please do not drive or operate heavy machinery while listening. Just relax into it.

There's no need to strain. . .just find your own level
with it. . .
And let your mind follow the rhythm of the breath. . .
And then. . .take a slow deep breath. . .
That fills your chest and abdomen. . .with an imaginary
ray of gentle calming light. . .
So that when you breathe out. . .you begin to let go
of any stress
That you've stored in your mind and body. . .
Just breathe out. . .and let it go. . .
And then take a second deep breath. . .
That fills your heart. . .with warm and loving feelings. . .
So that when you breathe out. . .you begin to release any
negative moods that keep you stuck. . .
Be expansive with it. . .and let go of what
you don't need. . .
And then take a third deep breath. . .that penetrates every
cell of your mind and body. . .
So that any tightness in your muscles. . .begins to shift and
free itself. . .
Just breathe out. . .let your shoulders drop. . .and let all
the tension go. . .
Just breathe into it
And as you let your breath begin to normalize. . .
Go deeper and deeper into relaxation. . .with each cycle
of breath. . .
So that the pace changes. . .and you begin to slow down. . .
And notice how it feels. . .to be calm and peaceful. . .
Where there's nothing to do. . .but to breathe normally
while you take time out. . .
Just breathe like this for a while. . .
And let the power of your breathing ease any
nervous tension. . .
Relax into it and go with the flow. . .
And now. . .
Imagine that you're going out for a walk. . .
In ideal weather. . .under a perfect sun. . .
No one is phoning or texting you. . .

Everyone is cared for and safe...
And as you stroll along...imagine that you come upon a
beautiful beach...
Where you decide to sit down, and gaze over at
the ocean waves...
And as you do this, begin to synchronize your breathing
to the rhythm of the ocean...
So that when you breathe in, it's like a wave refreshing
and restoring you...
And so that when you breathe out, it's like the wave
carries your troubles back out to sea...where they can
dissolve in the salt water...and be healed and transformed
into something more positive...or more adaptive...
Just breathe like this for a few breaths...
Let your breathing follow the rhythm of the sea...
And then let your thoughts and feelings join the rhythm of
the breath...
So that they begin to flow naturally...without any
resistance...
And as you do this...begin to distance yourself...
Where you can observe rather than getting caught up...
Just breathe...
And begin to gently detach from anything that's been
bothering you...
Let your thoughts and feelings come and go...
Without any resistance...
Breathe through it...
And as you contemplate a calm and peaceful synergy...
Imagine that a treasure box tumbles onto the shore
next to you...
Just observe it with mild curiosity...
And sense its familiarity...as though it's somehow
connected to you...
And as you do this...let go of any fear or doubts...
And just reach over and open the box...
Just begin to observe what's inside...
Without analyzing it...and without judgment...
Just notice what seems to stand out most...

Perhaps it's the very problem that's been on your mind...
Or a mood...or a feeling...or even a health symptom...
Just notice how you feel...as you gaze into the box...
And begin to contemplate the problem from this safe
emotional distance...
Just be with it like this...where you don't have to
struggle...but you can simply observe...
And then...imagine reaching in and removing that top
problem out of the box...
So that you can begin to see the feeling underneath it...
The one that keeps you emotionally stuck...or prevents
you from moving on in life...
Just observe with curiosity...and without judgment...
So that you can get a better handle on the problem...and
the feeling underneath it...
Just see it for what it is...and breathe through it...
And as you breathe...let your subconscious mind go
wherever it needs to...
To begin to free yourself from the emotional attachment
that keeps you stuck...
Just breathe through it...and let go...
And stay with it, for as long as you need to...
And then...imagine putting all the problems and the
feelings back into the box...
As you take it over to the shoreline...and watch it drift
gently back out to sea...
Just be willing to let go...and breathe through it...
And commit that feeling of letting go to your memory...
And as you farewell the struggle...prepare now to go
back to your normal day...
Knowing...that you can return to this inner
tranquility...whenever you want or need to...just
through the breath...
When you are ready...open your eyes...
And you may like to draw or write about whatever comes
to mind about this experience...

References

Achterberg, J. (2008). "Intentional healing: Consciousness and connection for health and well-being." Spoken word audio program. Louisville CO: Sounds True Audio Intentional Healing. Available at: www.soundstrue.com/store/intentional-healing.html, last accessed 2 February 2015.

Ackerberg, J., Dossey, B., and Kolkmeier, L. (1994). *Rituals of Healing: Using Imagery for Health and Wellbeing.* New York, NY: Bantam Books.

Allen, R.E. (1990). *The Concise Oxford Dictionary of Current English* (8th edition). Oxford: Oxford University Press.

Anderson, H. and Goolishian, H. (1998). "Human systems as linguistic systems: Evolving ideas about the implications for theory and practice." *Family Process 29,* 157–163.

Andresen, J. (2000). "Meditation meets behavioural medicine." *Journal of Consciousness Studies 7,* 17–73.

Anxiety Panic Hub (2010). Available at www.panicattacks.com.au/counsel/counsel.html, last accessed 2 February 2015.

Arnheim, R. (1969). *Visual Thinking.* Berkeley, CA: University of California Press.

Arnheim, R. (1992). "Why aesthetics is needed." *The Arts in Psychotherapy 19,* 149–151.

Australian Bureau of Statistics (ABS) (2012a). Mental and Behavioural Conditions. (Released 29th October 2012). Available at www.abs.gov.au/ausstats/abs@.nsf/Lookup/4338.0main+features192011-13, last accessed 18 May 2015.

Australian Bureau of Statistics (ABS) (2012b). Psychological Disability: Prevalence. (Released 9th February 2015). Available at www.abs.gov.au/ausstats/abs@.nsf/Latestproducts/4433.0.55.004Main%20Features52012?opendocument&tabname=Summary&prodno=4433.0.55.004&issue=2012&num=&view=, last accessed 18 May 2015.

Australian Bureau of Statistics (ABS) (2014). Australian Labour Market Statistics, July 2014: Retrenchments. (Released 8th July 2014). Available at www.abs.gov.au/ausstats/abs@.nsf/Latestproducts/6105.0Feature%20Article52July%202014?opendocument&tabname=Summary&prodno=6105.0&issue=July%202014&num=&view=, last accessed 18 May 2015.

Australian Bureau of Statistics (2008). *National Survey of Mental Health and Wellbeing of Australians: Summary of Results.* Canberra: ABS.

Badenoch, B. (2011). *The Brain-Savvy Therapist's Workbook (Norton Series on Interpersonal Neurobiology).* New York, NY: W.W. Norton and Company.

Baer, R.A., Smith, G.T., Hopkins, J., Krietemeyer, J., and Toney, L. (2006). "Using self-report assessment methods to explore facets of mindfulness." *Assessment 13*, 27–45.

Beck, A.T., Steer, R.A., and Brown, G.K. (1996). *Manual for the Beck Depression Inventory-II*. San Antonio, TX: Psychological Corporation.

Betensky, M.G. (1995). *What Do You See? Phenomenology of Therapeutic Art Expression*. London: Jessica Kingsley Publishers.

Betensky, M.G. (2001). "Phenomenological Art Therapy." In J.A. Rubin (ed.) *Approaches to Art Therapy: Theory and Technique* (2nd ed., pp. 121–133). New York, NY: Brunner-Routledge.

Bien, T. (2006). *Mindful Therapy: A Guide for Therapists and Helping Professionals*. Somerville, MA: Wisdom Publications.

Bishop, S.R., Lau, M., Shapiro, S., Carlson, L., *et al.* (2004). "Mindfulness: A proposed operational definition." *Clinical Psychology: Science and Practice 11*, 230–241.

Bodhipaksa, (2014). *Is Meditation about Making your Mind Go Blank?* Available at www.wildmind.org/background/making-the-mind-go-blank, last accessed 2 February 2015.

Borysenko, J. (2013, February 17). Available at https://www.facebook.com/joanborysenkocommunity/posts/10151494600982429, last accessed 2 February 2015.

Brown, K. and Ryan. R. (2003). "The benefits of being present: Mindfulness and its role in psychological well being." *Journal of Personality and Social Psychology 4*, 822–848.

Brown, K., Ryan, R., and Cresswell, J.D. (2007). "Mindfulness: Theoretical foundations and evidence for its salutary effects." *Psychological Inquiry 18*(4), 211–237.

Buie, D.H. (1981). "Empathy: Its nature and limitations." *Journal of the American Psychoanalytic Association 29*, 281–307.

Cahn, B.R. and Polich, J. (2006). "Meditation states and traits: EEG, ERP, and neuroimaging studies." *Psychological Bulletin 132*(2), 180–211.

Calvin (1996). *How Brains Think: Evolving Intelligence, Then and Now*. New York, NY: Basic Books.

Cane, D.K., Frank, T., Refsnes, K.C., Robinson, M.C., Rubin, J.A., and Ulman, E. (1983). "Roots of art therapy: Margaret Naumburg (1890–1983) and Florence Cane (1882–1952) – a family portrait." *American Journal of Art Therapy 22*(4), 111–123.

Chatzisarantis, N.L.D. and Hagger, M.S. (2007). "Mindfulness and the intention-behavior relationship within the theory of planned behavior." *PSPB 33*(5), 663–676.

Coryell, D.M. (2007). *Good grief: Healing through the Shadow of Loss*. Rochester, VT: Healing Arts Press.

Cozolino, L. (2002). *The Neuroscience of Psychotherapy*. New York, NY: Norton.

Davidson, R.J., Kabat-Zinn, J., Schumacher, J., Rosenkranz, M., Muller, D., Santorelli, S.F., *et al.* (2003). "Alterations in brain and immune function produced by mindfulness meditation." *Psychosomatic Medicine 65*, 564–570.

Davis, B. (2010). "Hermeneutic methods in art therapy research with international students." *The Arts in Psychotherapy 37*(3), 179–189.

Davis, B. (2011). "Contemplating panic: A case study in mindful art therapy." *Journal of Integrative Medicine 16*(2), 22–26.

Davis, B. (2012). "Hermeneutic methods in art therapy research and practice." (Webinar Course). American Art Therapy Association, Inc.: October 2012.

Davis, B., McGrath, N., Knight, S., and Davis, S.R. (2004). "'Aminina Nud Mulumuluna' (You gotta look after yourself): An evaluation of the use of art in health promotion for Aboriginal people in the Kimberley region of Western Australia." *Australian Psychologist 39*(2), 107–113.

Doidge, N. (2007). *The Brain that Changes Itself.* New York, NY: Penguin Group.

Dorjee, D. (2010). "Kinds and dimensions of mindfulness: Why it is important to distinguish them." *Mindfulness* (1), 152–160.

Dudgeon, P., Garvey, D. and Pickett, H. (2000). *Working with Indigenous Australians: A Handbook for Psychologists.* Perth, WA: Gunada Press.

Duits, R. (2004). "Heidegger and metaphysical aesthetics." *Postgraduate Journal of Aesthetics 1*(1), 18–24.

Eifert, G.H., McKay, M., and Forsyth, J.P. (2006). *ACT on Life, not Anger: The New Acceptance and Commitment Therapy Guide to Anger.* Oakland, CA: New Harbinger Publications, Inc.

Etkin, A., Egner, T. and Kalish, R. (2011). "Emotional processing in anterior cingulate and medial prefrontal cortex." *Trends in Cognitive Science 15*(2), 85–93.

Farb, N.A.S., Segal, Z.V., Mayberg, H., Bean, J., *et al.* (2007). "Attending to the present: Mindfulness meditation reveals distinct neural modes of self-reference." *Journal of Social, Cognitive, and Affective Neuroscience 2*, 248–258.

Fausek, D. (1997). *A Practical Guide to Art Therapy Groups.* Binghampton, NY: Harworth Press.

Fletcher, L.B., Schoendorff, B., and Hayes, S.C. (2010). "Searching for mindfulness in the brain: A process-oriented approach to examining the neural correlates of mindfulness." *Mindfulness* (1), 41–63.

Flynn, B. (2004). "Maurice Merleau-Ponty." *The Stanford Encyclopedia of Philosophy* (Summer 2004 edition). Available online at http://plato.stanford.edu/archives/sum2004/entries/merleau-ponty, last accessed 26 May, 2006.

Franklin, M. (1990). "The esthetic attitude and empathy: A point of convergence." *The American Journal of Art Therapy 29*(2), 42–47.

Franklin, M.B. (2001). "The artist speaks: Sigmund Koch on aesthetics and creative work." *American Psychologist 56*(2), 445–452.

Franklin, M. and Politsky, R. (1992). "The problem of interpretation: Implications and strategies for the field of art therapy." *The Arts in Psychotherapy 19*, 163–175.

Frost, S.B. (2010). *SoulCollage Evolving: An Intuitive Collage Process for Self-Discovery and Community.* Santa Cruz, CA: Hanford Mead Publishers, Inc.

Ganim, B. (1999). *Art and Healing: Using Expressive Art to Heal your Body, Mind, and Spirit.* New York, NY: Three Rivers Press.

Garai, J. (2001). "Humanist Art Therapy." In J.A. Rubin (ed.) *Approaches to Art Therapy: Theory and Technique* (2nd ed., pp. 149–162). New York, NY: Brunner-Routledge.

Gendlin, E.T. (1981/2007). *Focusing.* New York, NY: Bantam.

Hanh, T.N. (1976/1999). *The Miracle of Mindfulness* (2nd ed.). Boston, MA: Beacon Press.

Hanh, T.N. (2001). *Essential Writings: Modern Spiritual Masters Series*, (ed. R. Ellsberg), Maryknoll, NY: Orbis Books.

Hanson, R. (2009). *Buddha's Brain: The Practical Neuroscience of Happiness, Love, and Wisdom*. Oakland, CA: New Harbinger Publications, Inc.

Hanson, R. (2013). *Hardwiring Happiness: The New Brain Science of Contentment, Calm, and Confidence*. New York, NY: Harmony Books.

Harris, R. (2008). *The Happiness Trap: Stop Struggling, Start Living*. Auckland, NZ: Exile Publishing.

Harris, R. (2009). *ACT Made Simple*. Oakland, CA: Harbinger Publications, Inc.

Harris, R. (2012). *The Reality Slap: Finding Peace and Fulfillment When Life Hurts*. Oakland, CA: New Harbinger Publications, Inc.

Hayes, S.C. and Wilson, K.G. (2003). "Mindfulness: Method and process." *Clinical Psychology: Science and Practice 10*, 161–165.

Hayes, S.C., Strosahl, K., and Wilson, K.G. (1999). *Acceptance and Commitment Therapy: An Experiential Approach to Behavior Change*. New York, NY: Guilford Press.

Henderson, D.A. and Gladding, S.T. (1998). "The creative arts in counseling: A multicultural perspective." *Arts in Psychotherapy 25*(3), 183–187.

Holub, M. (2007). *Poems Before and After*. Northumberland: Bloodaxe Books Ltd.

Jung, G.C. (1964). *Man and his Symbols*. London: Picador.

Kabat-Zinn, J. (1990). *Full Catastrophe Living: Using the Wisdom of your Body and Mind to Face Stress, Pain, and Illness*. New York, NY: Delacorte.

Kabat-Zinn, J. (1994). *Wherever You Go, There You Are: Mindfulness Meditations in Everyday Life*. New York, NY: Hyperion.

Kaplan, F.F. (2000). *Art, Science and Art Therapy*. London: Jessica Kingsley Publishers.

Kashdin, T.B., and Ciarrochi, J. (2013). *Mindfulness, Acceptance and Positive Psychology: The Seven Foundations of Well-Being (The Mindfulness and Acceptance Practica Series)*. Oakland, CA: Context Press.

Kessler, R.C., Barker, P.R., Colpe, L.J., Epstein, J.F., *et al.* (2003). "Screening for serious mental illness in the general populations." *Archives of General Psychiatry 60*(2), 184–189.

Knill, P.J., Levine, E.G., and Levine, S.K. (2005). *Principles and Practice of Expressive Arts Therapy: Toward a Therapeutic Aesthetics*. London: Jessica Kingsley Publishers.

Kramer, E. (1987). "Sublimation and Art Therapy." In J.A. Rubin (ed.), *Approaches to Art Therapy* (26–43). New York, NY: Brunner/Mazel.

Kramer, E. (2000). *Art as Therapy*. London: Jessica Kingsley Publishers.

Kramer, G. (2007). *Insight dialogue: The Interpersonal Path to Freedom*. Boston, MA: Shambhala.

Lamb, K. and Howland, L. (1995). *The Art of Conversation: The Perfect Icebreaker*. Kangaroo Flat, Australia: Louise Howland.

Landgarten, H. (1975). "Adult art psychotherapy." *Art Psychotherapy 2*, 65–76.

Langer, E. (2005). *On Becoming an Artist: Reinventing Yourself through Mindful Creativity*. Ballantine Books: 2005.

Lark, C.V. (2005). "Using art as language in large group dialogues: The TREC Model." *Art Therapy 22*(1), 24–31.

Levine, E.G. (2005). "The Practice of Expressive Arts Therapy: Training, Therapy and Supervision." In *Principles and Practice of Expressive Arts Therapy: Toward a Therapeutic Aesthetics* (171–199). London: Jessica Kingsley Publishers.

Levine, P. (2010). *An Unspoken Voice: How the Body Releases Trauma and Restores Goodness.* Berkley, CA: North Atlantic Books.

Levine, S.K. (2005). "The Philosophy of Expressive Arts Therapy: Poïesis as a Response to the World." In *Principles and Practice of Expressive Arts Therapy: Toward a Therapeutic Aesthetics.* (15–74). London: Jessica Kingsley Publishers.

Lichtenberg, J.D., Lachmann, F.M., and Fosshage, J.L. (1992). *Self and Motivational Systems: Toward a Theory of Psychological Technique.* Hillsdale, NF: The Analytic Press.

Liebowitz, M. (1999). *Interpreting Projective Drawings: A Self-Psychological Approach.* Philadelphia, PA: Brunner/Mazel.

Linehan, M.M. (2014). *Cognitive-Behavioral Treatment of Borderline Personality Disorder, Second Edition.* New York, NY: Guilford.

Linesch, D. (1994). "Interpretation in art therapy research and practice: The hermeneutic circle." *Arts in Psychotherapy 21*(3), 185–195.

Lovibond, S.H. and Lovibond, P.F. (1995). *Manual for the Depression Anxiety Stress Scales* (2nd ed.). Sydney: Psychology Foundation Monograph.

Lusebrink, V.B. (2004). "Art therapy and the brain: An attempt to understand the underlying processes of art expression in therapy." *Journal of the American Art Therapy Association 21*(3), 125–135.

Maclagan, D. (2001). *Psychological Aesthetics.* London: Jessica Kingsley Publishers.

Malchiodi, C.A. (2003). *Handbook of Art Therapy.* New York: NY, Guildford Press.

Maslow, A.H. and Maslo, B.G. (1971/1993). *The Farther Reaches of Human Nature.* New York, NY: Penguin Group.

McKenzie, S. and Hassed, C. (2012). *Mindfulness for Life.* Auckland, NZ: Exisle Publishing.

McNiff, S. (1998). *Art-Based Research.* London: Jessica Kingsley Publishers.

McNiff, S. (2004). *Art Heals: How Creativity Cures the Soul.* Boston, MA: Shambhala.

Merleau-Ponty, M. (1945/1964). *The Phenomenology of Perception* (trans. J. Edie). Evanston, IL: North Western University Press.

Mikulas, W.L. (2011). "Mindfulness: Significant common confusions." *Mindfulness, 2,* 1–7.

Naumburg, M. (1953). *Psychoneurotic Art: Its Function in Psychotherapy.* New York, NY: Grune and Stratton.

NCCAM, (2014). *Complementary, Alternative, or Integrative Health: What's In a Name?* Available at: http://nccam.nih.gov/health/whatiscam, last accessed 18 May 2015.

National Institute of Mental Health (NIMH) (2014). *Psychotherapies.* Available at www.nimh.nih.gov/health/topics/psychotherapies/index.shtml, last accessed 18 May 2015.

Ogden, P., Minton, K. and Pain, C. (2006). *Trauma and the Body: A Sensory Approach to Psychotherapy.* (series editor, Daniel J. Siegel, M.D.). New York, NY: W.W. Norton and Company.

Oyan, S. (2003). In D. Goleman (1997). *Healing Emotions: Conversations with the Dalai Lama on Mindfulness, Emotions, and Health.* Boston, MA: Shambhala.

Palmer, R.E. (1969). *Hermeneutics.* Evanston, IL: Northwestern University Press.

Palmer, R.E. (1971). "Phenomenology" – Edmund Husserl's article for the Encyclopaedia Britannica (1927). *Journal of the British Society for Phenomenology, 2,* 77–90.

Pennebaker, J.W. (2004). *Writing to Heal: A Guided Journal for Recovering from Trauma and Emotional Upheaval.* Oakland, CA: New Harbinger Publications, Inc.

Peterson, B. (1998). *Learning to See Creatively.* New York, NY: Amphoto.

Porges, S. (2011). *The Polyvagal Theory: Neurophysiological Foundation of Emotions, Attachment, Communication and Self-Regulation.* New York, NY: W.W. Norton and Company.

Potter-Efron, R. and Potter-Efron, P. (1989). *Letting Go of Shame.* Centre City, MN: Hazelden.

Ramachandran, V.S. and Blakeslee, S. (1998). *Phantoms in the Brain: Probing the Mysteries of the Human Mind.* New York, NY: William Morrow.

Rappaport, L. (2014). *Focusing Oriented Art Therapy: Accessing the Body's Wisdom and Creative Intelligence.* Philadelphia, PA: Jessica Kingsley Publishers.

Rennie, D.L. (2002). "Experiencing Psychotherapy: Grounded Theory Studies." In D.J.E. Cain (ed.), *Humanistic Psychotherapies: Handbook of Research and Practice.* (117–144). Washington, DC: American Psychological Association.

Richardson, W. J. (1967). *Heidegger: Through Phenomenology to Thought.* (2nd ed.). The Hague: Martinus Nijhoff.

Rogers, C.R. (1961). *On Becoming a Person* (pp.163–182 and 347–359). Boston, MA: Houghton Mifflin Company.

Rogers, C.R. (1980). *A Way of Being.* Boston, MA: Houghton Mifflin Company.

Rogers, N. (1993). *The Creative Connection: Expressive Arts as Healing.* Palo Alto, CA: Science and Behavior Books.

Rogers, N. (2001). "Person-Centered Expressive Arts Therapy." In J.A. Rubin (ed.) *Approaches to Art Therapy: Theory and Technique* (2nd ed.) (163–175). New York, NY: Brunner-Routledge.

Rubin, J.A. (1984). *The Art of Art Therapy.* New York, NY: Brunner/Mazel Publishers.

Rubin, J.A. (1987/2001). *Approaches to Art Therapy: Theory and Technique* (2nd ed.). New York, NY: Brunner-Routledge.

Rubin, J.A. (2005). *Artful Therapy.* Hoboken, NJ: John Wiley and Sons.

Segal, Z.V., Williams, J.M.G., and Teasdale, J.D. (2002). *Mindfulness-Based Cognitive Therapy for Depression: A New Approach to Preventing Relapse.* New York, NY: Guilford Press.

Seligman, M.E.P. and Csikszenmihalyi, M. (2000). "Positive psychology: An introduction." *American Psychologist 55,* 5–14.

Siegel, D. J. (2007): "Mindfulness training and neural integration." *Journal of Social, Cognitive, and Affective Neuroscience 2,* 259–263.

Siegel, D.J. (2007). *The Mindful Brain: Reflection and Attunement in the Cultivation of Well-Being (Norton Series on Interpersonal Neurobiology).* New York, NY: W.W. Norton and Company, Inc.

Siegel, D.J. (2009). "Mindful awareness: Mindsight, and neural integration." *The Humanist Psychologist 37*(2). 137–158.

Siegel, D.J. (2010). *Mindsight: The New Science of Personal Transformation.* New York, NY: W.W. Norton and Company.

Siegel, D J. (2010). *The Mindful Therapist: A Clinician's Guide to Mindsight and Neural Integration.* (Norton Series on Interpersonal Neurobiology). New York, NY: W.W. Norton and Company.

Siegel, D.J. (2012). *Pocket Guide to Interpersonal Neurobiology: An Integrative Handbook of the Mind* (Norton Series on Interpersonal Neurobiology). New York, NY: W.W. Norton and Company.

Silverman, R.H. (2001). *Exploring the Values of Art.* Available at, http://instructional1.calstatela.edu/laa/personal-psych_2.html, last accessed February 5, 2007.

Solso, R.L. (1994). *Cognition and the Visual Arts.* Cambridge, MA: MIT Press.

Spinelli, E. (2005). *The Interpreted World: An Introduction to Phenomenological Psychology* (2nd ed.). London: Sage Publications.

Teasdale, J.D., Segal, Z.V., Williams, J.M.G., Ridgeway, V.A., Soulsby, J.M., and Lau, M.A. (2000). "Prevention of relapse/recurrence in major depression by mindfulness-based cognitive therapy." *Journal of Consulting and Clinical Psychology 68*, 615–623.

Terwee, S.J.S. (1990). *Hermeneutics in Psychology and Psychoanalysis.* Berlin: Springer-Verlag.

Thomson, I.D. (2011). *Heidegger, Art, and Postmodernity.* Cambridge, UK: Cambridge University Press.

Van Manen, M. (1990/2006). *Researching Lived Experience: Human Sciences for the Action Sensitive Pedagogy,* (2nd ed.). New York, NY: SUNY Press.

Wadeson, H. (1973). "Separateness." *Art Psychotherapy 1,* 131–133.

Walsh, R. and Shapiro, S.L. (2006). "The meeting of meditative disciplines and western psychology: A mutually enriching dialogue." *American Psychologist 61*(3), 227–239.

What is meditation? Available at: http://thebuddhistcentre.com/text/what-meditation, last accessed August 9, 2013.

Williams, M., Teasdale, J., Segal, Z., and Kabat-Zinn, J. (2007). *The Mindful Way through Depression.* New York, NY: Guilford Press.

Winnicott, D.W. (1971). *Playing and Reality.* New York, NY: Routledge.

Subject Index

Author Index